PROBLEMS OF RELIGIOUS PLURALISM

PROBLEMS OF RELIGIOUS PLURALISM

John Hick

St. Martin's Press   New York

St. Martin's Press, Inc., 175 Fifth Avenue, New York, NY 10010
Printed in Hong Kong
Published in the United Kingdom by The Macmillan Press Ltd.
First published in the United States of America in 1985

ISBN 0-312-65154-6

Library of Congress Cataloging in Publication Data
Hick, John.
Problems of religious pluralism
Includes index.
1. Religious pluralism – Addresses, essays, lectures.
2. Religion – Philosophy – Addresses, essays, lectures.
I. Title.
BL85.H45   1985   291.1'72   85–2505
ISBN 0-312-65154-6

*To friends who are prophets of religious pluralism
within their several traditions*

*Masao Abe within Buddhism,
Hasan Askari within Islam,
Ramchandra Gandhi within Hinduism,
Kushdeva Singh within Sikhism,
Wilfred Cantwell Smith within Christianity,
and Leo Trepp within Judaism*

Contents

Preface

Western philosophy of religion has until very recently operated almost entirely within the horizons of the Judaeo-Christian tradition. Religious problems have meant the problems of monotheism: how to prove, probabilify, or otherwise show it to be reasonable to believe in, the existence of God; how to meet the challenges posed to theism from modern linguistic philosophy and from modern science; how to respond in theistic terms to the ancient problem of evil; and so on. And the solutions proposed have accordingly been relevant only within a monotheistic universe of discourse.

This work should and will of course continue, and interesting new developments will from time to time occur. But the larger and more radical development is the expansion of the subject into an intercultural discipline. For the philosophy of religion is in principle the philosophy of all forms of religion and not only of that which one either participates in or has reacted against. And so the post-World War II explosion of information about the history and phenomenology of religions has begun to tempt or challenge philosophers of religion to look at their subject in the context of the religious life and beliefs of the human race as a whole.

As one philosopher's first steps in this new world of thought the papers in this book are exploratory and tentative. The opening chapter has a different character from the rest in that it is autobiographical, describing three controversies encountered on the way towards a global perspective. No one should inflict personal stories on anyone who does not wish to hear them, and this chapter is entirely optional; nothing will be lost from the later more philosophical discussions by skipping this opening piece. On the other hand a philosopher is a human being, living through the history of his or her time, and it may be of interest to some to see another small example of the way in which life influences and is influenced by thought.

The second chapter, 'Seeing-as and Religious Experience', begins to develop in the direction of religious pluralism a theme that I have explored before in purely Judaeo-Christian terms, namely the application of Wittgenstein's concept of seeing-as to the analysis of religious experience and faith. Chapter 3, 'A Philosophy of Religious Pluralism', moves to a general interpretation, from a religious point of view, of the plurality of the great religious traditions. This chapter was contributed to a volume in honour of one of the leaders of thought in this area, Wilfred Cantwell Smith, recently retired from Harvard University. Chapter 4, 'Religious Pluralism and Absolute Claims', which includes some discussion of the distinctively Christian problem of Christology, was contributed to a series of colloquia on cultural pluralism and religious belief held by the Boston University Institute for Philosophy and Religion in 1981. This series is only one of a number of academic conferences in recent years devoted to aspects of religious pluralism in the United States, where the subject is at present receiving more attention than in Europe.

'On Grading Religions' (Chapter 5) engages with one of the major problems of religious pluralism, and the next two chapters, 'On Conflicting Religious Truth-Claims' and 'In Defence of Religious Pluralism', are responses to critics of this and other articles. May I say again that I am extremely grateful to those who from time to time engage in constructive debate with me. I have learned much from them and expect to learn more in the future.

Chapter 8, 'Eschatological Verification Reconsidered', takes a theme on which I have written before and begins to detach it from a purely Christian setting; and the last chapter, 'Present and Future Life', likewise seeks to open out the question of human destiny as a global issue.

These chapters are preliminary to a more comprehensive and systematic volume which will appear in a few years time. It is hoped that any critical responses that the present book may be fortunate enough to elicit will help in the writing of the larger work.

Department of Religion   JOHN HICK
Claremont Graduate School
Claremont, California

1 Three Controversies*

This august body has asked me to take my turn in providing an autobiographical evening, and I am dutifully doing so. And when I consider what, if anything, may have been of theological interest in my life I find that it can only be the controversies, which have (thus far) been principally three in number. It may surprise you that one whom you have, I trust, found to be of a mild and inoffensive disposition should ever have been involved in any controversies, and should even have come to be seen by some as dangerously radical and extreme. I suppose that this has been made possible by an inner conflict between instinct and intellect. By instinct I am conservative, cautious, timid and credulous. But my intellect has nevertheless led me to various conclusions which do not fit well with such a temperament; and it is these conclusions that have got me into trouble. Left to itself my essentially conservative nature would probably have enabled me to be a thoroughly respectable theologian and churchman, upholding every current consensus. Indeed I started well enough, and kept to the straight and narrow path for a number of years. But eventually the mind showed a certain wilful propensity to philosophy, and to the asking of questions, together with an unsociable habit of noticing flaws in arguments and inconsistencies in accepted belief-systems and, to make matters worse, an obsessive respect for facts. All this, alas, has almost entirely undermined my erstwhile respectability and has led to the incidents I am about to relate.

The first controversy was basically absurd, happening as it did in the middle of the twentieth instead of the nineteenth century, although we now find that more than twenty years later the same anachronistic criticisms are directed in England against David Jenkins, Bishop of Durham. I moved in 1959 from Cornell University to Princeton Theological Seminary, and thought it

* A paper delivered to the Pacific Coast Theological Society at Berkeley, California, in 1983.

appropriate to transfer my ministerial membership from the Presbytery of Berwick in England to the local presbytery of the United Presbyterian Church, the Presbytery of New Brunswick. Its membership included a strong fundamentalist minority, and it so happened that the chairman of the Committee on Candidates and Credentials, concerned with ministerial transfers, was a leader of this group. He had been a disciple of Henry Machen, a notable fundamentalist theologian of the previous generation who had written about the virgin birth and had left Princeton Seminary in disgust as a result of controversy concerning it. The former gentleman exercised his right to ask the question – a tactless question, you may think, in the middle of the twentieth century – whether there was anything in the Westminster Confession of 1647 to which I took exception. The Westminster document does of course contain a number of items which any of us in this room would certainly regard as open to question, and I mentioned several, such as the six-day creation of the world, the predestination of many to eternal hell, the verbal inspiration of the Bible, and the virgin birth of Jesus. It was this last that caused the fundamentalists to rebel against the Presbytery's vote in April 1961 to accept me as a member. I did not deny the doctrine, but on the other hand did not positively affirm it. I was agnostic about its historical truth, and held that in any case it is not an essential item of Christian faith. In adhering to this position in spite of the fact that it proved so troublesome I had both positive and negative motives: positively, a belief that theologians, like other citizens, should be expected to tell the truth and, negatively, a dislike of the way in which the fundamentalists were able to induce some of our Seminary students to pretend to be more traditionally orthodox than they really were, and perhaps even more – let me confess it – by dislike of the way they were trying to do the same to me.

The Complaint of eighteen ministers and elders against my reception into the Presbytery was heard nearly a year later, in March 1962, by the Judicial Commission of the Synod of New Jersey, and to the surprise and dismay of many of us it was sustained. I was thus no longer a Presbyterian minister, and presumably no longer eligible to hold the office of Stuart Professor of Christian Philosophy at the Seminary, which is owned by the Church. When the Synod's decision was announced, various newspapers called for a comment and I offered this statement:

The theological question at issue is whether every Presbyterian minister must affirm a biological miracle in connection with the birth of Christ, or whether this is a secondary matter about which it is possible for some of us to be uncertain. I distinguish between the central Christian faith in the Incarnation, and the theologically peripheral story of the Virgin Birth, and following St Paul, St John, St Mark and most of the other New Testament writers, I do not found my belief in the Incarnation upon the Virgin Birth tradition. I would therefore not exclude from the Presbyterian ministry those who decline to make the Christian Gospel stand or fall on something inessential, and I anticipate that when this matter is finally decided by the General Assembly of our church, the broader view will prevail.

In order to bring the dispute before the General Assembly another Complaint had to be launched, appealing in turn against the Synod's action. The first signatory was our pastor, Ben Anderson, the minister of the Princeton Witherspoon church. Witherspoon was a 95-per-cent black congregation, originally consisting of the slaves whose owners worshipped not far away in the First Presbyterian Church. The congregation included at that time three or four white families, of which we were one, attracted by the quality of worship at this church. In the services there was an almost palpable sense, seldom alas found in our large and more affluent congregations, of participation in a greater and sacred reality.

The Synod's barring of me from Presbytery membership was for a while an item of ecclesiastical news and the Seminary had to face publicity which some welcomed and others resented. But the basic position of the Seminary, among both faculty and students, was one of active support, regardless of whether individuals did or did not themselves accept the virgin-birth doctrine. I received a number of welcome supporting letters from theologians, including one from a present member of this Society, John Bennett, then Dean of Union Seminary, New York. There were also of course numerous hostile letters, some reasoned and capable to being replied to, others anonymous and emotionally poisoned, assuring me of the writer's entire contempt and a future place in hell. A few even qualified for my Psycho-ceramic or Crack-pot file.

However, I could not help being conscious throughout that this was a basically ridiculous rumpus. I see from my file that I replied to John Bennett, 'I very much appreciate your kind note. It seems to me pathetic that the Christian Church should be wasting its time and energies on this issue at this time of day, but I have no doubt that the matter will be properly sorted out in due course.' I was in fact confident that the appeal on my behalf to the General Assembly would succeed, because otherwise the Church would become torn by heresy hunts in which fundamentalists in every Presbytery would be able to challenge any minister on the question of the virgin birth. And so I was not at all surprised when the Permanent Judicial Commission of the General Assembly, meeting at Denver, Colorado in May 1962, decided Administrative Case no. 4 in favour of the Complainants, thereby overturning the Synod's action and reinstating the Presbytery's. What the General Assembly decided was that each Presbytery has the right to exercise its own judgement in accepting or rejecting candidates for membership. It held that a higher Church court should only review such a decision on 'the most extraordinary grounds'; and by implication it declared that a failure to affirm the doctrine of the virgin birth did not constitute such a ground.

The whole incident had now taken well over a year. Its results were, I think, that the principle of toleration on subsidiary theological issues was reaffirmed by the Church; that conservative pressures upon more liberal theological students were a little harder to apply; and that the image of Princeton Seminary was slightly changed for the better from the point of view of the more liberal sections of the Church. The Seminary was still basically highly orthodox; but so at that time was I, so that I felt at home in it. Certainly our move in 1974 to Cambridge University had nothing to do with the virgin-birth controversy. We are all liable to make moves from time to time in the course of our careers, and to an Englishman Cambridge had a powerful attraction.

The Cambridge University Divinity School was then in an extremely lively and interesting period under the Regius Professorship of Dennis Nineham. But I was a Lecturer (in American terms, perhaps associate professor) in the Philosophy of Religion and naturally wanted sooner or later to occupy one of the few full Chairs in the subject in the country; and when in 1967 the H. G. Wood Chair at Birmingham University became vacant I applied for it and was appointed. I knew little about Birmingham at that time but it turned out to be a fascinating and challenging place. In particular it was, and is, a racially, culturally and religiously pluralistic city, about a tenth of whose 1 million inhabitants are black – in the contemporary sense in which black includes brown. During the 1950s and 1960s there was a considerable immigration into Britain from the Indian sub-continent and the West Indies, bringing large numbers of people from the Commonwealth to become part of the population of Britain. At the time when they came they were needed, mainly to do some of the rougher jobs in a then-expanding economy; and Birmingham was one of the main centres of this black and brown immigration. There were, and are, both religious and political aspects to this new diversity. Religiously the immigrants were Muslims from Pakistan and, later, Bangladesh; Sikhs from the Indian Punjab; Hindus from Gujerat and other parts of India; and fervent Pentecostal Christians from Jamaica, Trinidad and the other Caribbean islands.

I shall return to the religious pluralism presently. The political issues arose from the ethnic and cultural mix in explosive interaction with a pervasive racism which had become deeply ingrained in the British mind during the centuries of imperialism. Only seventy or so years earlier, in the latter years of the reign of Queen Victoria, Britain had been at the centre of an Empire comprising nearly a quarter of the land-mass of the earth and a quarter of its population. The younger sons of upper- and middle-class English families had for generations gone overseas to rule over millions of subjects, nearly all of whom were black or brown. Now it is a sad fact of human nature that one who is set over other people without their consent will almost inevitably come to think of his subjects as basically inferior to himself. Otherwise, why would he be ruling over them? And this all-too-natural syllogism of the imperialist mind operates even when the rule is to some extent benevolent. And so there grew up the almost universally acepted dogma, whether or not formulated as such, of the inherent superiority of the white person and the correlative inferiority of the black, brown and yellow peoples of Africa, India and the Far East. Naturally, this negative perception of black people in the colonies had a certain self-fulfilling power. They were generally, as a matter of policy, educated for an inferior role and, until the independence movements attained a sufficient popular momentum, were conditioned to see this as their natural status.

The shadow of this long colonial history fell across London and Birmingham and the other British cities in which the new immigrants were settled, in a prejudice against them which was expressed in widespread and effective discrimination in employment, housing, education, medical and other welfare services, and in the practice of their religions. The official policies of successive post-war governments, in most areas other than immigration itself, were in principle non-discriminatory; but the actual situation on the ground was one of pervasive colour discrimination. In response to this a number of both official and voluntary organisations emerged in which white and black liberals and (as the Establishment would say) radicals sought to counter discrimination and to promote a more just and equal society. In Birmingham, besides being a member of one of the official such bodies – which was not however, in my view, meeting the needs of the situation adequately – I was also one of the founders and the first chairman of a voluntary group, called All Faiths for One Race, AFFOR for short. The real founder was the very dynamic and talented young 'radical' who served as its first Director. The management committee consisted of Christians, Muslims, Jews, Hindus, Sikhs, and yet others who were humanists and Marxists. We received grants from various trusts, and over the years AFFOR has done an enormous amount of valuable work in a number of related areas: assisting people of the ethnic minorities to find their way through the intricacies of the welfare state; helping local Muslim groups to obtain planning permission to convert houses into mosques; educational work in schools and colleges; seeking appropriate local radio time for the minorities; trying to influence the churches towards greater involvement in the struggle for a successful multi-cultural and multi-faith Britain; research into the special needs of the elderly and the handicapped among the ethnic minorities and work with the appropriate local government authorities on these matters; and so on. But there were also more explosive issues, which have taken up a good deal of AFFOR's time and energies – helping young West Indians in their often stormy and sometimes violent relations with the police, and combating the influence of explicitly racist political organisations, of which the two most prominent in the 1960s and 1970s were the National Front and the National Party. Like the Nazis in Germany in the 1930s they blamed society's economic and social problems upon a visible and vulnerable scapegoat minority, in this case the blacks, and preached hatred against them and advocated their deportation.

They also provided a violent outlet for the energies of youths whose minds they had distorted by this propaganda of hate. Their public meetings and processions often precipitated a wave of violent incidents – bricks flung through Asian shop-windows, muggings of blacks and Asians ('Paki-bashing'), and sometimes swastikas painted on synagogue walls and Jewish cemeteries. Those who opposed them did so at the risk of violence to themselves. For example, our AFFOR director was physically assaulted whilst handing out anti-National Front leaflets and – such was sometimes the attitude of the police – had to defend himself in court against a charge of incitement to violence! With the support of various advisers from the Law Faculty at Birmingham University he was acquitted. Again, the very dedicated and brave Jewish investigative journalist whose researches provided the ammunition for an AFFOR pamphlet, to which I will come in a moment, was viciously attacked and wounded with a knife at a demonstration in London. But his researches had made it well known in anti-racist circles, although still little known among the general public, that these racist movements had explicitly Nazi roots. Ever since World War II the same small group had been active in the leadership of a series of organisations with such names as the British National Party, the League of Empire Loyalists, and the Racial Preservation Society, and they were now leading the National Front and the National Party. In the past they had openly worn Nazi uniforms, they had each year celebrated Hitler's birthday, and they were still publishing Nazi literature, including virulently anti-Jewish leaflets. Several of them had prison records for violent racist activities. For example, a chairman of the National Front had been imprisoned after leading a rally at which he declared that 'the Jew is like a poisonous maggot feeding on a body in an advanced state of decay'. And the chairman of the National Party, speaking at a rally just after the murder of an Asian youth in London in 1976, had shouted, 'One down, a million to go.' He was, incidentally, acquitted on a charge of incitement to racial hatred by a judge who though that black people ought to be able to take such remarks with good humour.

It was in this same year, 1976, that I undertook to produce an AFFOR pamphlet, addressed to the Christian churches, detailing the alarming background information that we had from the Jewish journalist whom I have mentioned and from other sources about the National Front and National Party leadership. I carefully checked all the information and was able to list the past convictions of these men as well as quoting from internal documents revealing their sinister political aims. Our idea was to invite the local church-leaders in the Birmingham area to write a short preface commending the pamphlet to their people, thus getting their churches involved in one of the most fundamental moral issues affecting the life of many British cities. The then Anglican Bishop of Birmingham (not the present Bishop, Dr Hugh Montefiore) agreed in principle to join with other church leaders in such a preface, and the preface was drafted. However the Bishop's legal adviser urged him not to associate himself with such a publication, and in particular not to name names or mention criminal convictions. He cited the Rehabilitation of Offenders Act of 1974, which limited the circumstances in which it is permissible to refer to spent convictions. If we transgressed these limits we should be liable to be sued by the individuals named. However, our own legal advisers told us that there was indeed a possibility that we might be sued for defamation by any of the individuals named, but that we should have a good defence; for the Act did not remove in such a case as this the existing justifications of truth and fair comment. We therefore decided to go ahead and to welcome a court action, if one was brought, as a way of giving further publicity to the facts concerning these racist organisations. But we could not get the church-leaders to contribute a preface. Some (the Methodist leadership, for example) wanted to help, but were not able to build a common front. There were long negotiations back and forth which held up publication for many weeks; and at one point the idea was even mooted of two editions, one to be published by the local Council of Churches with a preface by the church-leaders, but omitting the passages which named names, and another with the full text, to be published by AFFOR. But in the end even this was not acceptable to the church-leaders, who were no doubt fearful of the divisive effects, within churches as affected by racist sentiment as the rest of the population, of a controversial move on this issue. So strong was this negative point of view among the ecclesiastical establishment that one very senior and respected churchman saw the pamphlet as 'an essay in character assassination' which would only make people sympathise with the National Front and National Party leaders and so be counterproductive! But there is no doubt in my own mind that these church-leaders, in their anxiety to avoid unpleasant controversy and in their reluctance to get mixed up in the harsh realities of political action, had their heads firmly buried in the ground. The National Front and National Party leaders had not in the least repented of their Nazi past, and were still engaged in the same blatantly racist and anti-Semitic propaganda, to the peril of black and Jewish citizens and of the peace of society. Further, they were presenting their racism – as such people so often do – as a defence of Christian civilisation! It would have been highly appropriate for church-leaders to criticise them publicly and wholeheartedly.

In the end we had to go beyond our local church-leaders, and an excellent Preface was provided by Colin Morris, a Christian leader well known for his opposition to racism. He happened that year to be President of the Methodist Conference but had to write his Preface as an individual rather than in his official capacity.

And so the pamphlet was published, under the title *The New Nazism of the National Front and National Party. A Warning to Christians*. It received wide attention in church circles and was several times reprinted, coming as it did at the right time to influence opinion in the British churches. A number of people were then trying to turn the churches against racism and our pamphlet aided their efforts. The racist leaders who were named in it did not take legal action against us, calculating no doubt that this could only further harm them. Instead of a writ, all that I received was a shower of hostile letters, including an anonymous letter of the kind that was familiar to everyone whom the National Front identified as an enemy. It was part of their technique to show that they knew one's home address and to remind one that violence was part of their stock in trade. The letter ended, 'Race traitors like you had better keep away from us Wog killers.'

The late 1970s were something of a turning-point in the mobilisation of Christian opinion in Britain against organised racism, and saw a growing commitment to the creation of a just pluralistic society. This new consciousness among British Christians has gone on growing, although even now it only affect a minority within the churches. Connected with it is a new openness to people of other faiths and a new interest in Islam, Judaism, Sikhism, Hinduism and Buddhism. This new attitude has had all sorts of practical implications, not least in education. At the same time that I was chairman of AFFOR, I was also chairman of the

Religious and Cultural Panel of the Birmingham Community Relations Committee, the latter being an official body set up by the Government. This panel called for a new Syllabus of religious education for the city. I should explain that in Britain religious education is compulsory within the State-school system and is taught in accordance with an Agreed Syllabus which is created for each area by a statutory conference consisting of representatives of the Church of England, the other Protestant churches, the teachers' organisations, and the local education authority. The existing Birmingham Syllabus was of the traditional kind – exclusively Christian and consisting largely of Bible study. Since there were now many classes in inner-city schools in which the majority of the children were not Christians but positive adherents of some other faith, a new multi-faith syllabus was urgently needed. The city authorities took up the suggestion, and agreed to include among the non-Anglican church representatives a Roman Catholic, a Jew, a Muslim, a Hindu and a Sikh. I was asked to serve on the statutory conference and to chair the co-ordinating committee which organised and oversaw its work. This took hundreds of hours over a period of several years, but in the end we produced a new Agreed Syllabus in which each child (in the schools in which it is effectively implemented) learns about more than one faith whilst being able to specialise in his or her own. That this was possible, in an operation requiring the co-operation of so many different interests, is an indication of the changing attitude of the host community to people of other faiths. And, more broadly, I think it would be true to say that among the minority of church people who are aware of and concerned about Britain's new religious pluralism there is an open and accepting spirit and a real desire to seek justice. In practice it is accepted that the other great streams of religious life and thought are independently valid areas of divine revelation and salvation, and that the traditional policy of seeking to convert all mankind to the Christian way should be abandoned. In the experience of meeting people of other faiths many Christians have thus been led by the Spirit into significantly new attitudes and practices.

But at the same time theological understanding has lagged behind this new practical outlook. Most Christians still adhere to the traditional theology according to which there is only one way of salvation, from which there follows the duty to try to bring all human beings into that way. The old conception of the unique superiority and sole saving-power of Christianity is still enshrined in liturgies and hymns, and sounds from time to time through the customary Sunday rhetoric. Thus many Christians find themselves behaving in one way whilst still thinking theologically in another. And it has been one of my vocations as a theologian to work for the new kind of theology of religions which is implied by the new praxis. This seems to me to involve a frank recognition that there is a plurality of divine revelations and contexts of salvation. But such a pluralistic view inevitably has implications for Christology, and this brings me to the third of my three controversies.

This has centred on the doctrine of the Incarnation, a doctrine which has long been especially cherished by the Anglican mind and imagination. Stirred by the problem of religious pluralism to consider the logical character of incarnational language, I had come to the conclusion that the Incarnation should be understood as a symbolic or metaphorical or mythic rather than as a literal truth. Others in the English theological world, coming along the paths of New Testament and Patristic study, had arrived at essentially the same position. Two colleagues at Birmingham University, teaching the New Testament and Patristics, had concluded out of their historical work that the idea that Jesus was God incarnate, or the Second Person of a divine Trinity living a human life, is a construction of the Church suggested by themes that were present in the Jewish and Greek traditions and with many partial analogues in other expressions of religious thought in the ancient Mediterranean world. In addition to them there was the Patristic scholar and systematic theologian Maurice Wiles, Regius Professor of Divinity at Oxford and former chairman of the Church of England's Doctrinal Commission, and the New Testament scholar Dennis Nineham, then Warden of Keble College, Oxford, and formerly Regius Professor of Divinity at Cambridge. We were later joined by Don Cupitt, Dean of Emmanuel College, Cambridge, and Leslie Houlden, then Principal of Cuddesdon Anglican Theological College, near Oxford. The seven of us agreed to attempt a volume of essays which we eventually called *The Myth of God Incarnate*, published in 1977, with myself functioning as editor; and we met about twice a year to discuss our draft chapters as they progressed. The three themes running through the book are (1) the historical thesis that Jesus did not teach that he was in any sense God incarnate and had no

conception of himself as the Second Person of a divine Trinity; (2)
that it is possible to trace a development during the decades after
Jesus's death from the view of him as a prophet appointed by God
in the last days to usher in the Kingdom to the properly
incarnational doctrine which was finally established at the
Councils of Nicaea and Chalcedon in the fourth and fifth
centuries; and (3) my own special concern, that to see the
language of divine incarnation as metaphorical, or mythic, makes
it possible for Christians to come to a genuine acceptance of
religious pluralism. The theological world had of course been
familiar with the two historical theses for a century or more, and
the third thesis was by no means a new one; so that members of
this Society may well be surprised that the book caused such a
furor. It did however strike a very sensitive nerve of British church
life. It was widely reported, and discussed in the national
newspapers. The religious press was full of it for several weeks.
The *Church Times* ran the headline 'Seven against Christ?' The
word 'heresy' was freely used. The Sunday after publication a
preacher in St Paul's Cathedral declared that the *Myth* authors
should consider whether they are still Christians. In the Synod of
the Church of England, which happened to be in session when the
book was published, we were likened, by the person appointed to
lead the prayers, to the German Christians who supported Hitler!
The *Sunday Telegraph* published a picture of Christ on the cross,
with a copy of our book nailed above his head. The Greek
Orthodox Archbishop of Great Britain declared that the authors
of *The Myth* 'have fallen prey to an opposition of a demonic
character'. A counter-book called *The Truth of God Incarnate* was
rapidly produced, edited by a leading member of the evangelical
wing of the Church of England. A pamphlet was published by the
Church of England Evangelical Council, calling upon the Anglican members of our team to resign their orders; and there was a
call by the Moderator of the Church of Scotland for me, as a
Presbyterian, to do likewise. On the other hand, the Archbishop
of Canterbury, Donald Coggan, refrained from joining the outcry
against my Anglican colleagues; and neither my own church, the
United Reformed Church, nor the Methodist Church, of which
one of the seven is a member, made any move against us, either
nationally or locally – although there was considerable discussion, sometimes heated, within both.

The explanation for this furor lies I think partly in the

distinctive ethos of Anglicanism, in which the imagery of Incarnation has long been deeply embedded, and, as a corollary of this, in a gap in the Anglican world – but by no means only the Anglican world – between scholarly research and parish preaching. Anglican scholars have of course been as aware as anyone else of the historical implausibility of the older view that Jesus presented himself as God incarnate; but nevertheless the people in the parishes were generally quite unprepared to hear this said openly and its implications discussed. And it was the fact that some of the people who were now saying it were from the 'top drawer of Anglican scholarship' that made it impossible to keep the issue out of the limelight. We were much criticised for using so provocative a title as *The Myth of God Incarnate*. And indeed it is true that the title was more provocative than the book itself, which was written in a sober scholarly vein and was indeed much too heavy-going for the average occupant of the church pews. But if the book had come out under a dull title, such as *Studies in the Concept of Incarnation in the Patristic Period*, as an expensive hard-cover volume addressed to the scholarly world, it would have made virtually no contribution to the growth of Christian understanding. For its thought was already familiar to and largely accepted within the scholarly world; what was needed was something that would make the body of church people and the general public aware of the historical and theological issues.

I think that on the whole the book has in fact served its purpose well. It succeeded in communicating widely, going to over 30,000 copies in a few months. A follow-up volume, *Incarnation and Myth*, was published two years later, based on a conference in Birmingham between the *Myth* authors and some of the book's critics. Since then a number of more recent British writings on Christology have taken *The Myth* as their starting-point and have been able to advance through the door which it opened. My own view is that the cat of historical criticism which was let out of the bag to public view can never be put back again, and that theological writers and preachers in Britain are now much less likely to use the traditional 'Son of God', 'God incarnate' language as though its meaning were clear and unproblematic. And the realisation that religious language expresses our apprehension of the divine in mythic pictures, and that these pictures are human and culturally conditioned, has opened up for some the possibility that the different mythologies of the great religious traditions may constitute alternative, or perhaps even complementary, rather than rival ways of picturing the divine reality.

But there is nevertheless a real problem, or tension, inherent in this kind of theological work. The religious life is lived largely in terms of symbol and myth. And the Christian myth of the descent of the eternal Son of God into our human world, being born of a virgin, dying in agony on the cross in atonement for our sins, and rising glorified into heaven, has an imaginative unity and an emotional and moral impact which have powerfully affected millions of people over many centuries. We can dismantle the myth, and speak instead of Jesus as a man who was startlingly open to God, and who saved people by making real to them the divine presence and the transforming divine claim upon their lives, thus setting up a new way of salvation within human history – the way of discipleship to Jesus as he is mediated to us through the Bible and the Church. Such a demythologised Christianity has the advantages that it is in continuity with the religious message and impact of Jesus himself, that it is historically honest and realistic, and that it is compatible with genuine religious pluralism. But on the other hand it has the disadvantage that it does not really require or therefore sustain the magic and mystery, the bright colours and warm feelings and deep mythic resonances of Christmas and Easter, which constitute an important imaginative and emotional dimension of the religious life of very many people. When Jesus was alive, and again to a lesser extent in the presence of any of the saints among his disciples, people have been and are so immediately conscious of God, and of the divine will that is to be done in the present moment, that they do not need a mythology to support them. But Christianity as a continuing social reality, providing a framework for the life of whole populations, does need a mythology. And, unless and until a new mythology emerges, the old one will continue. In the meantime we have to live in a certain tension, which is sometimes a painful tension and which can only be avoided at the cost of cutting oneself off from one or other of its two sources. One can cut oneself off from the life of the Church, with its liturgies and rituals and festivals and poetry expressing the traditional mythology, a mythology which has indeed become a part of one's own life; or one can cut oneself off from the insistent claims of rationality and from one's awareness of the universality of the divine presence and activity, transcending our own particular mythology. But for my part I don't want to cut myself off from either. I prefer to continue to live in the tension between them, hoping for God's grace and illumination.

2 Seeing-as and Religious Experience*

Much has been written during the last twenty years or so under the stimulus of Wittgenstein's remarks on religion. Indeed we have in the writings of D. Z. Phillips and others what is often referred to as the neo-Wittgensteinian philosophy of religion, according to which religious language constitutes an essentially autonomous 'language-game' with its own internal criteria of truth, immune to challenge or criticism from those who do not participate in that language-game. From a religious point of view it is an attractive feature of this position that it acknowledges the right of the believer to his/her beliefs and practices. On the other hand, however, in doing this it (in my view) cuts the heart out of that religious belief and practice. For the importance of religious beliefs to the believer lies ultimately in the assumption that they are substantially true references to the nature of reality; and the importance of religious practices to the practitioner lies in the assumption that through them one is renewing or deepening one's relationship to the transcendent divine Reality. The cost, of course, of making such metaphysical claims in the secular world of today is that they inevitably provoke controversy; and a corresponding benefit of the contrary view is that such controversy is avoided. Thus, when a Humanist or a Marxist tells a believer that it is foolish to pray to God, because there is no God to pray to, the neo-Wittgensteinian philosopher of religion will tell both atheist and believer that they are playing different language-games and that there can be no proper ground of controversy between them. The believer is thus left secure in his or her belief, protected from outside attack, but

* Reprinted, with permission, from the *Proceedings of the Eighth International Wittgenstein Symposium* (Vienna: Hölder-Pichler-Tempsky, 1984), held by the Österreichische Ludwig Wittgenstein Gesellschaft at Kirchberg-am-Wechsel, Austria, in August 1983.

only on the understanding that such beliefs do not depend for their validity upon the universe being structured in one way (a theistic way) rather than another (an atheistic way).

I am personally not convinced that Wittgenstein, were he alive today, would have endorsed this neo-Wittgensteinian development. I have the impression that he respected ordinary life and speech too much to accept a theory which so blatantly contradicts the normal intentions of most religious-language users. To deny, for example, that the language of petitionary prayer is normally meant to presuppose the reality of a divine being who exists in addition to all the human beings who exist, is (in my view) to contradict the operative meaning of such language. Convictions about the character of the universe, and hence about the most appropriate way to live in it, are turned by this neo-Wittgensteinian analysis into expressions of emotion and attitude whose appropriateness depends upon their expressing the feelings and attitudes of the religious person rather than upon their being appropriate to the nature and structure of reality independently of human feelings and attitudes. It is true that religious people commonly use language in metaphorical ways, and indeed that religious pictures of the universe are typically mythological in character, so that their affirmations concerning God, creation, judgement, heaven and hell, and so on are generally to be construed as pointers rather than as literal descriptions. But the pointers are undoubtedly intended to point to realities transcending the metaphors and myths; and to suppress this intention is to do violence to religious speech and to empty the religious 'form of life' of its central and motivating conviction. This does not seem to me to be in the spirit of Wittgenstein. However I may be mistaken about this. I would accordingly only say that, in my view, the neo-Wittgensteinian philosophy of religion embodies a misinterpretation of religion, and *possibly* also a misinterpretation of Wittgenstein's utterances on religion.

There is however another aspect of Wittgenstein's work that has, I believe, constructive implications for the philosophy of religion. This is his discussion of 'seeing-as' and related topics in the second part of the *Philosophical Investigations*. I want to suggest that this helps us to place the distinctively religious way of experiencing life on the epistemological map as a form of what I shall call 'experiencing-as'; and helps us to understand religious faith, in its most basic sense, as the interpretative element within this distinctively religious way of experiencing life. I shall not attempt to extract a doctrine from Wittgenstein's pages, but attempt only to show how his thought can be fruitful in ways which he himself may or may not have had in mind. I leave the question of the extent to which Wittgenstein would have approved or disapproved this suggestion to others who are more fully conversant with the Wittgenstein corpus. Such a procedure is perhaps in line with his own words in the Foreword to the *Investigations*: 'I should not like my writing to spare other people the trouble of thinking. But, if possible, to stimulate someone to thoughts of his own.'

First, then, I suggest that Wittgenstein was right in the implicit judgement, which pervades his references to religion, that what is important and to be respected here is not the conventional religious organisations and their official formulations but the religious way of experiencing and participating in human exis- tence and the forms of life in which this is expressed. It is in relation to this 'religious way of experiencing life and of participat- ing in human existence' that the concept of seeing-as is relevant. Wittgenstein's Cambridge disciple John Wisdom opened a window in this direction in some informal remarks which I heard him address to the Socratic Society in Oxford around 1949. This was before the publication of the *Investigations*, although there had been a reference to the idea of seeing-as in the *Brown Book*; but in any case I presume that Wisdom's wider use of the concept had been stimulated by discussions with Wittgenstein himself.

Wittgenstein points to two senses of the word 'see'. If I am looking at a picture, say the picture of a face, in sense number one I see what is physically present on the paper – mounds of ink, we might say, of a certain shape, size, thickness and position. But in sense number two I see the picture of a face. We could say that in this second sense to 'see' is to interpret or to find meaning or significance in what is before us – we interpret and perceive the mounds of ink as having the particular kind of meaning that we describe as being the picture of a face, a meaning that mounds of ink, simply as such, do not have. The interpretative activity which is integral to 'seeing' in this second sense, but which is absent from 'seeing' in the first sense, is particularly evident when we are looking at a puzzle picture. As Wittgenstein says, 'we *see* it as we interpret it'.[1] As he also puts it, in seeing-as an element of thinking is mixed with pure 'seeing' in the first sense. When we see the

duck–rabbit picture as a duck and then as a rabbit Wittgenstein
speaks of these as aspects, and he says that 'the flashing of an
aspect on us seems half visual experience, half thought'.[2]

We can, I suggest, immediately expand the concept of seeing-
as, based only on sight, into the comprehensive notion of
experiencing-as. For the finding of meaning does not occur only
through sight. We can hear a sound as that of a passing train; feel
the wood as bamboo; smell the cloud as smoke; taste what is in our
mouth as peppermint. In our everyday perception of our environment we use several sense-organs at once; and I suggest that
we adopt the term 'experiencing-as' to refer to our ordinary
multi-dimensional awareness of the world. Like seeing-as (or
'seeing' in the second sense), experiencing-as involves thought in
the form of interpretation, i.e. becoming aware of our environment in terms of the systems of concepts embodied in what
Wittgenstein sometimes called language-games. He points out
the important fact that the capacity to apply concepts to percepts
is a necessary condition for having certain kinds of experience
(such as seeing a particular triangle on paper as suspended from
its apex) but not for having certain other kinds, such as feeling a
toothache.[3]

The distinction between experiencing and experiencing-as, like
that between seeing and seeing-as – or 'seeing' in the first sense
and in the second – is however seldom actually exemplified. For
we hardly ever experience, as distinguished from experiencing-as.
Even so stark an experience as feeling pain is often linked by
conceptual filiaments with the systems of meaning that structure
our lives. Pain can be experienced as a threat to our holiday plans,
career, financial security, and so on. Perhaps in very early infancy
there is entirely unconceptualised experience. And perhaps there
are kinds of aesthetic experience which are not forms of
experiencing-as. But I think it is safe to say that ordinary human
experiencing is always experiencing-as, always a perceiving of
that which is present to us as having a certain recognisable
character, which I am calling its meaning or significance. I take it
that one of Wittgenstein's basic insights was that the system, or
(perhaps better) the living organism, of meanings in terms of
which we live is carried in the language of a certain linguistic
community.

Wittgenstein himself seems to have been inclined to restrict the
notion of seeing-as to manifestly ambiguous cases, such as puzzle

pictures. It would not, he says, make sense for me 'to say at the sight of a knife and fork "Now I am seeing this as a knife and fork." . . . One doesn't *"take"* what one knows as the cutlery at a meal *for* cutlery.'[4] On the other hand he recognises that there are occasions when I would not say '*I* am seeing this as an *x*', but when nevertheless someone else might properly say of me, '*He* is seeing that as an *x*.' And this is true, I would suggest, even of the ordinary everyday seeing-as, or experiencing-as, in which we recognise familiar objects such as knives and forks. If a stone-age savage is shown the cutlery he will not see it as cutlery because he lacks the concepts, which are part of our culture but not of his, of cutlery, knife, fork, and so on, together with such other surrounding concepts as eating at table with manufactured implements. We could therefore say of him, 'He is not experiencing it as cutlery' – but, perhaps, as something utterly puzzling or maybe as a set of magical objects. And in contrast we could say of a member of our own culture, 'He/she *is* seeing it as cutlery.'

I therefore hold that, apart perhaps from certain marginal cases, all human experiencing is experiencing-as. And I would further suggest – in general conformity, I think, with Wittgenstein's insights – that the awareness of entities as having this or that kind of significance always has a practical dispositional aspect. To experience the thing on the table as a fork is to be in a dispositional state to behave in relation to it in a certain range of ways, namely those that consist in using it as a fork. And in general to perceive what is before us as an *x* is to be in a state to treat it as an *x* rather than as a *y* or a *z*.

We next have to notice that in addition to the kinds of meaning exhibited by individual physical objects, such as knives and forks, ducks and rabbits, people and books, there are the more complex kinds of meaning exhibited by situations. 'Situation' is a relational notion. A situation, for X, consists of a set of objects which are unified in X's attention and which have as a whole a practical dispositional meaning for X which is more than the sum of the meaning of its constituent objects. Thus our present situation in this session this morning can be described in purely physical terms, corresponding to reports of what is seen in Wittgenstein's first sense. Here we would describe each physical object in the room, including both human bodies and inanimate furniture, and their several shapes, sizes, positions and movements. But another kind of report is also possible, using such higher-level concepts as

Gesellschaft, philosophy, discussion, academic paper, criticism, and so forth. Human consciousness normally functions at this situational level, and it is here that we find the distinctively human dimensions of meaning over and above those that we share with the other animals.

These distinctively human dimensions of meaning or significance, transcending the purely physical meaning of our environment, appear to be of three kinds – ethical, aesthetic and religious. I shall say a little about ethical meaning, very little about aesthetic meaning, and then rather more about religious meaning.

The ethical or moral meaning that we may experience a situation as having could also be called its social or its personal significance. For morality has to do with the interactions and relationships between persons. A purely physical account of a situation involving people would include a number of mobile organisms; but at the personal or ethical level we interact with these organisms as persons – as centres of consciousness, feeling, will – beings whose very existence imposes a potential moral claim upon us. For example, suppose I am present at a street accident in which someone is struck by a car and is now lying in the road bleeding and in pain. If we can imagine someone experiencing this situation purely at the physical level of meaning they would observe the body and the flowing blood and hear the cries and moans; and that would be all. But as ethical beings we are also conscious in all this of a fellow human being in pain and danger, urgently needing first aid. We are perceiving ethical meaning, experiencing the situation not only in natural but also in moral terms. And the practical–dispositional aspect of this form of experiencing-as is expressed in the action which our distinctively moral awareness renders appropriate – in this case to do whatever we can to help the injured person.

Clearly, ethical presupposes natural meaning and can in this precise sense be described as a higher order of meaning. For ethical meaning is always the further meaning or meta-meaning of a physical situation. And to experience a situation as having this or that kind of moral significance is to be in a dispositional state to behave within it in a way or ways appropriate to its having that significance. These dispositional responses may of course be weakened or cancelled out by some contrary self-regarding concern. But to be a moral, as distinguished from an amoral, being is to be conscious of ethical obligations, whether or not or to whatever extent one's actions are guided by them. And to say that we are moral creatures is to say that we are liable to experience human situations as having this kind of significance.

Aesthetic meaning sometimes presupposes physical meaning (as in paintings of natural scenes and of people), but sometimes seems not to (as in much music and in abstract art). And to experience something as having aesthetic significance sometimes has a practical–dispositional aspect, affecting our attitudes, and sometimes seems not to but to be purely contemplative. The varieties and complexities here are daunting, and I do not propose to enter upon them. But to say that human beings are aesthetic as well as ethical creatures is to say that they are liable to experience aspects of their environment as having aesthetic significance.

Moving now to religious meaning, to describe *homo sapiens* (as has often been done) as the religious animal is to say that human beings have apparently always displayed a tendency to experience individuals, places and situations as having religious meaning. Throughout a good deal of religious life individuals have been experienced as divine – usually kings, as in many primitive societies and in ancient Egypt (where the Pharaoh was divine), ancient Babylon (where the king embodied divine power), and ancient Israel (where the king was adopted at his enthronement as 'son of God'); and in Christianity Jesus of Nazareth is seen and devotionally experienced as divine. Many places have been identified as sacred – for example, hills, mountains, streams and rocks among many primitive societies, and within the great world religions such places as Benares (Varanasi), Bodh-Gaya, Jerusalem, Bethlehem, Mecca, Lourdes, and other places of pilgrimage. But the kind of experiencing-as that I should like more particularly to consider is situational. It is a feature of monotheistic religion that any human situation may, in principle, be experienced as one in which one is living in the unseen presence of God. For God is omnipresent, and in all that one does and undergoes one is having to do with God and God with oneself. In the case of saints this consciousness of existing in God's presence has been relatively continuous and pervasive; in the case of more ordinary believers it is occasional and fleeting. In the Hebrew scriptures a particular thread of history is described throughout in religious terms. The escape of a band of alien slaves from Egypt and their wanderings in the Sinai desert and eventual settlement in Canaan, their national consolidation and subsequent conquest and dispersion, are all presented as God's dealings with his chosen people. Their political ups and downs are seen as his encouragement of them when they were faithful and disciplining of them when unfaithful. This is often referred to as the prophetic interpretation of Hebrew history. But this interpretation is not, or not basically, a theoretical interpretation, a historical schema imposed retrospectively upon the events of the past. It has its origin in the experience and then the preaching of the prophets concerning the meaning of events that were currently taking place around them. To give just one example, when in the time of Jeremiah a hostile Chaldean army was investing Jerusalem, to the prophet this was God wielding a foreign power to punish his erring people. As one well-known commentary says, 'Behind the serried ranks of the Chaldean army [Jeremiah] beheld the form of Jahweh fighting for them and through them against His own people.'[5] Jeremiah did not, I take it, literally see the visible form of Yahweh; but he did experience what was taking place as having the religious meaning of divine punishment. And it is this kind of experience reported by the prophets that, in Jewish understanding, provides the clue to the meaning of all history.

Again, the New Testament centres upon the disciples' experience of Jesus as the Christ, the Messiah, God's anointed agent to bring in the Kingdom. In experiencing Jesus as the Messiah the disciples were experiencing him in a way that was significantly different from that of those who perceived him, for example, as a heretical rabbi or a political agitator; and the New Testament documents reflect this apostolic interpretation of Jesus as the Christ.

This word 'interpret' can function in two senses or on two levels; and we should now distinguish them. There is the second-order sense in which an historian interprets the data, or a detective the clues, or a lawyer the evidence, or indeed in which a metaphysician may interpret the universe. This is a matter of conscious theory-construction. At this second-order level there are religious interpretations or, as we call them, theologies and religious philosophies, consisting in metaphysical theories which offer interpretations of the universe, in which the data of religious experience are given a central and controlling place. Wittgenstein seems to have regarded these – rightly, in my view – as much less important than the religious experiencing of life, and than the dispositional aspect of this in attitudes of trust and acceptance and in acts of worship and service. For this second-order kind of interpretation presupposes the more basic, or first-order, inter- pretative activity which enters into virtually all conscious experi- ence of our environment. In this first-order sense we are interpreting what is before us when we experience this as a fork, that as a house, and the other as a cow, or again, when we experience our present situation as one of participating in a session of philosophical discussion; or again, when some of us might, in a moment of reflection, be conscious in and through this same situation of being at the same time in the presence of God. Interpreting in this sense is normally an unconscious and habitual process resulting from negotiations with our environment in terms of the set of concepts constituting our operative world of meaning. To interpret in this primary sense involves, as I suggested earlier, being in a dispositional state to behave in ways appropriate to the perceived meaning of our situation. Thus, in the case of the Chaldean threat to Jerusalem, the appropriate response was one of national repentance; and it was to this that Jeremiah called his fellow citizens. In the case of the disciples' experience of Jesus as the Messiah, their dispositional response was one of reverence and obedience, of openness to his teachings and of radical readiness to change their lives in following him.

We observe in these examples that that which is religiously interpreted and experienced is in itself ambiguous – in this respect like a puzzle picture – in that it is also capable of being perceived non-religiously. A secular historian, describing the events recorded in the Hebrew scriptures, would speak of the rise and fall of empires, and of economic, political and cultural pressures, and so forth, but would not speak of God as an agent in ancient Near Eastern history. Likewise, in addition to those who experienced Jesus as the Christ there were others who perceived him under quite other categories; so that the Jesus-phenomenon was capable of being perceived in these contrary ways. One can see very clearly in such a case the hierarchy of interpretations that can occur. At the most basic level there was awareness of the physical existence of Jesus as a living organism. Superimposed upon this there was, at the human and social level of awareness, Jesus's life as a human being interacting with others in the Palestinian society of his day. And superimposed upon this there was, for the specifically Christian mode of experiencing-as, Jesus as the Christ. At this third level the Jesus-phenomenon was importantly ambiguous, capable of being experienced in a number of different ways, as the Messiah, as a prophet, as a rabbi, and so on. This ambiguity is characteristic of religious meaning. On a larger scale we can say that the world, or indeed the universe, is religiously ambiguous – able to be experienced by different people, or indeed by the same person at different times, in both religious and naturalistic ways. This is not of course to say that one way of experiencing it may not be correct, in the – perhaps un-Wittgensteinian – sense of being appropriate to its actual character, and the other incorrect. But, if so, the true character of the universe does not force itself upon us, and we are left with an important element of freedom and responsibility in our response to it. From a religious point of view this connects with the thought that God leaves us free to respond or fail to respond to him. I would suggest that this element of uncompelled interpretation in our experience of life is to be identified with faith in the most fundamental sense of that word. All forms of experiencing-as embody cognitive choices and are thus acts of faith; and religious faith is that cognitive choice which distinguishes the religious from the secular way of experiencing our human situation. This element of cognitive freedom in relation to God has been stressed by many religious thinkers. For example, Pascal, speaking of the incarnation, says,

> It was not right that he should appear in a manner manifestly divine, and completely capable of convincing all men; but it was also not right that he should come in a manner so hidden that he could not be recognized by those who sincerely seek him. He has willed to make himself perfectly recognizable by those; and thus, willing to appear openly to those who seek him with all their heart, and hidden from those who flee from him with all their heart, he so arranges the knowledge of himself that he has given signs of himself, visible to those who seek him, and not to those who do not seek him. There is enough light for those who only desire to see, and enough obscurity for those who have a contrary disposition.[6]

It should be noted that this account of faith as an uncompelled interpretation or mode of experiencing-as is neutral as between religious and secular understandings. The theist and the atheist might agree to this epistemological analysis of faith whilst making their own different cognitive choices, the believer trusting that the religious way of experiencing-as into which he or she has entered will ultimately be vindicated by the future unfolding of the character of the universe.

A point which Wittgenstein would, I imagine, want to stress is that the way in which we experience our environment depends upon the system of concepts that we use and that this is carried from generation to generation in the language in terms of which we think and behave. There is thus a relativity of forms of experience to what Wittgenstein sometimes called language-games or, as I should prefer to say, cultures. This helps to explain how it is that there is not just one form of religious experiencing-as, with its own superstructure of theological theories, but a plurality, which we call the different religions. Given the concept of God – that is, the concept of the ultimate reality and mystery as personal – and given a spiritual formation within a theistic tradition, the religious person is likely to experience life as being lived in the unseen presence of God, the world around one as God's creation, and moral claims as divine commands. Such a person may be, for example, a Jew or a Christian or a Muslim or a Sikh or a theistic Hindu. But, given the very different concept of Brahman, or of the Dharma, or Śūnyatā, or the Tao – that is, a concept of the ultimate reality and mystery as the non-personal depth or ground or process of existence – and given a spiritual formation within a non-theistic tradition the religious person is likely to experience life as the karmic process leading eventually to enlightenment and the realisation of reality. Such a person may be, for example, an advaitic Hindu or a Theravāda or Mahāyāna Buddhist. Thus, if we ask why it is that Christians, Buddhists, Jews, Muslims, Hindus report such different perceptions of the divine, the answer that suggests itself is that they are operating with different sets of religious concepts in terms of which they experience in characteristically different ways. This is of course a neutral account of the situation. It could be that the religions are all experiencing erroneously, projecting different illusions upon the universe. And it could on the other hand be that they are each responding to an infinite divine reality which exceeds our human conceptualities and which is capable of being humanly thought and experienced in these fascinatingly divergent ways.

My suggestion, then, is that Wittgenstein's concept of seeing-as, enlarged into the concept of experiencing-as, applies to all our conscious experience of our environment, including the religious ways of experiencing it. Such a view does justice to the systematically ambiguous character of the world, capable as it is of being experienced both religiously and naturalistically. These are radically different forms of experiencing-as. Such a view also does justice to the fact that the religious experiencing of life can itself take different forms. The world may be experienced as God's handiwork, or as the battlefield of good and evil, or as the cosmic dance of Shiva, or as the beginningless and endless interdependent process of *pratītya samutpāda* within which we may experience *nirvāṇa*; and so on. These are different forms of religious experiencing-as. Thus Wittgenstein's original concept can be fruitful in perhaps unexpected ways when it is brought into connection with the concrete religious forms of life.

NOTES

1. Ludwig Wittgenstein, *Philosophical Investigations*, trs. G. E. M. Anscombe (Oxford: Basil Blackwell, 1953) p. 193.
2. Ibid., p. 197.
3. Ibid., p. 208.
4. Ibid., p. 185.
5. John Skinner, *Prophecy and Religion* (Cambridge University Press, 1922) p. 261.
6. Pascal, *Pensées*, Brunschviecg edn, no. 430, trans. F. W. Trotter (London: J. M. Dent, 1932; New York: E. P. Dutton, 1932).

3　A Philosophy of Religious Pluralism*

Wilfred Cantwell Smith in his work on the concepts of religion and of religions has been responsible, more than any other one individual, for the change which has taken place within a single generation in the way in which many of us perceive the religious life of mankind.

Seen through pre-Cantwell Smith eyes there are a number of vast, long-lived historical entities or organisms known as Christianity, Hinduism, Islam, Buddhism, and so on. Each has an inner skeletal framework of beliefs, giving shape to a distinctive form of religious life, wrapped in a thick institutional skin which divides it from other religions and from the secular world within which they exist. Thus Buddhism, Islam, Christianity, and the rest, are seen as contraposed socio-religious entities which are the bearers of distinctive creeds; and every religious individual is a member of one or other of these mutually exclusive groups.

This way of seeing the religious life of humanity, as organised in a number of communities based upon rival sets of religious beliefs, leads to the posing of questions about religion in a certain way. For the beliefs which a religion professes are beliefs about God, or the Ultimate, and as such they define a way of human salvation or liberation and are accordingly a matter of spiritual life and death. Looking at the religions of the world, then, in the plural we are presented with competing claims to possess the saving truth. For each community believes that its own gospel is true and that other gospels are false in so far as they differ from it. Each believes that the way of salvation to which it witnesses is the authentic way, the only sure path to eternal blessedness. And so the proper question in face of this plurality of claims is, which is the true religion?

* Reprinted, with the publisher's permission, from *The World's Religious Traditions: Essays in Honour of Wilfred Cantwell Smith*, ed. Frank Whaling (Edinburgh: T. & T. Clark, 1984).

In practice, those who are concerned to raise this question are normally fully convinced that theirs is the true religion; so that for them the task is to show the spiritual superiority of their own creed and the consequent moral superiority of the community which embodies it. A great deal of the mutual criticism of religions, and of the derogatory assessment of one by another, has been in fulfilment of this task.

This view of mankind's religious life as divided into great contraposed entities, each claiming to be the true religion, is not however the only possible way of seeing the religious situation. Cantwell Smith has offered an alternative vision.

He shows first that the presently dominant conceptuality has a history that can be traced back to the European Renaissance. It was then that the different streams of religious life began to be reified in Western thought as solid structures called Christianity, Judaism, and so forth. And having reified their own faith in this way Westerners have then exported the notion of 'a religion' to the rest of the world, causing others to think of themselves as belonging to the Hindu, or the Confucian, or the Buddhist religion, and so on, over against others. But an alternative perception can divide the scene differently. It sees something of vital religious significance taking different forms all over the world within the contexts of the different historical traditions. This 'something of vital religious significance' Cantwell Smith calls faith. I would agree with some of his critics that this is not the ideal word for it; for 'faith' is a term that is more at home in the Semitic than in the Indian family of traditions and which has, as his own historical researches have shown, become badly over-intellectualised. But I take it that he uses the term to refer to the spiritual state, or existential condition, constituted by a person's present response to the ultimate divine Reality. This ranges from the negative response of a self-enclosed consciousness which is blind to the divine presence, whether beyond us or in the depths of our own being, to a positive openness to the Divine which gradually transforms us and which is called salvation or liberation or enlightenment. This transformation is essentially the same within the different religious contexts within which it occurs: I would define it formally as the transformation of human existence from self-centredness to Reality-centredness. This is the event or process of vital significance which one can see to be occurring in individuals all over the world, taking different forms within the contexts of the different perceptions of the Ultimate made available by the various religious traditions.

These cumulative traditions themselves are the other thing that one sees with the aid of the new conceptuality suggested by Cantwell Smith. They are distinguishable strands of human history in each of which a multitude of religious and cultural elements interact to form a distinctive pattern, constituting, say, the Hindu, Buddhist, Confucian, Jewish, Christian or Muslim tradition. These traditions are not static entities but living movements; and they are not tightly homogeneous but have each become in the course of time internally highly various. Thus there are large differences between, for example, Buddhism in the time of Gautama and Buddhism after the development of the Mahāyāna and its expansion northwards into China; or between the Christian movement in Roman Palestine and that in medieval Europe. And there are large differences today between, say, Zen and Amida Buddhism in Japan, or between Southern Baptist and Northern Episcopalian Christianity in the United States. Indeed, since we cannot always avoid using the substantives, we might do well to speak of Buddhisms, Christianities, and so on, in the plural. A usage consonant with Cantwell Smith's analysis has however already become widespread, and many of us now often prefer to speak not of Christianity but of the Christian tradition, the Hindu tradition, and so on, when referring to these historically identifiable strands of history.

These cumulative traditions are composed of a rich complex of inner and outer elements cohering in a distinctive living pattern which includes structures of belief, life-styles, scriptures and their interpretations, liturgies, cultic celebrations, myths, music, poetry, architecture, literature, remembered history and its heroes. Thus the traditions constitute religious cultures, each with its own unique history and ethos. And each such tradition creates human beings in its own image. For we are not human in general, participating in an eternal Platonic essence of humanity. We are human in one or other of the various concrete ways of being human which constitute the cultures of the earth. There is a Chinese way of being human, an African way, an Arab way, a European way, or ways, and so on. These are not fixed moulds but living organisms which develop and interact over the centuries, so that the patterns of human life change, usually very slowly but sometimes with startling rapidity. But we are all formed in a hundred ways of which we are not normally aware by the culture into which we were born, by which we are fed, and with which we interact.

Let us then enter, with Cantwell Smith, into the experiment of thinking, on the one hand, of 'faith', or human response to the divine, which in its positive and negative forms is salvation and non-salvation and, on the other hand, of the cumulative religious traditions within which this occurs; and let us ask what the relation is between these two realities – on the one hand salvation/liberation and on the other the cumulative traditions.

In various different forms this question has been much discussed within the Christian world, particularly during the last hundred and fifty years or so as Christians have become increasingly conscious of the continuing reality of the other great religious traditions. For this period has seen renaissances within the Hindu and Buddhist worlds – to an important extent, it would seem, in reaction to eighteenth- and nineteenth-century Christian imperialism – and a resurgence of Islam is currently taking place. These developments have precipitated intense debate among Christian thinkers in which many different options have been and are being canvassed. Both because of the fullness of this discussion within Christianity, and because I am myself a Christian and am concerned with the problem from a Christian point of view, I propose to describe the main options in Christian terms. They are three in number.

The first, which we may call 'exclusivism', relates salvation/ liberation exclusively to one particular tradition, so that it is an article of faith that salvation is restricted to this one group, the rest of mankind being either left out of account or explicitly excluded from the sphere of salvation. The most emphatic and influential expression of such a faith occurred in the Catholic dogma *Extra ecclesiam nulla salus* (outside the Church, no salvation) and the corresponding assumption of the nineteenth-century Protestant missionary movement: outside Christianity, no salvation. In these developments Christian thought went beyond a mere overlooking of non-Christian humanity – which might perhaps simply be attributed to restricted vision – to a positive doctrine of the unsaved status of that wider human majority. Exclusiveness of this strong kind was supported by a juridical conception of salvation. If salvation consists in a change of status in the eyes of God from the guilt of participation in Adam's original sin to a forgiveness made possible by Christ's sacrifice on the cross, the appropriation of which is conditional upon a personal response of faith in Christ, this salvation can very naturally be seen as restricted to the Christian faith community. If on the other hand salvation is understood as the actual transformation of human life from self-centredness to Reality-centredness, this is not necessarily restricted within the boundaries of any one historical tradition. One cannot know *a priori* where or to what extent it occurs; one can only look at the living of human life in its endlessly varied circumstances and try to discern the signs of this transformation. Except in those whom we call saints, in whom the transformation is sufficiently advanced to be publicly evident, such discernment is often extremely difficult; for salvation/liberation, understood in this way, is to be found in many stages and degrees in the varying qualities of true humanity, often realised more in some areas of life than in others, and with advances and regressions, efforts and lapses in all the respects in which human beings develop and change through the experience of life in time. There may of course – as the Hindu and Buddhist traditions generally teach – be a final moment of enlightenment in which the transformation is completed and Reality-centredness definitively supersedes the last remnants of self-centredness. But, even if this should be a universal pattern, the journey leading towards that final moment must be long and slow; and progress on the journey can to some extent be humanly discerned as the process of salvation gradually taking place. This understanding of salvation/liberation as the actual transformation of human beings is more easily open than is the juridical understanding of it to the possibility that the salvific process may be taking place not only within one tradition but within a number of traditions.

Christian exclusivism has now largely faded out from the 'mainline' churches, but is still powerful in many of the 'marginal' fundamentalistic sects; and it should be added that the 'margins' of Christianity are probably more extensive today than ever before.

However, we may now turn to a second Christian answer to our question, which can be labelled 'inclusivism'. This can be expressed in terms either of a juridical or of a transformation-of-human-existence conception of salvation. In the former terms it is the view that God's forgiveness and acceptance of humanity have been made possible by Christ's death, but that the benefits of this sacrifice are not confined to those who respond to it with an explicit act of faith. The juridical transaction of Christ's atone-ment covered *all* human sin, so that all human beings are now open to God's mercy, even though they may never have heard of Jesus Christ and why he died on the cross of Calvary. I take it that it is this form of inclusivism that the present Pope was endorsing in his first encyclical when he said that 'man – every man without any exception whatever – has been redeemed by Christ, and because with man – with each man without any exception whatever – Christ is in a way united, even when man is unaware of it'.[1] This statement could however also be an expression of the other form of Christian inclusivism, which accepts the under-standing of salvation as the gradual transformation of human life and sees this as taking place not only within Christian history but also within the contexts of all the other great world traditions. It regards this however, wherever it happens, as the work of Christ – the universal divine Logos, the Second Person of the divine Trinity, who became incarnate in Jesus of Nazareth. Thus we can speak of 'the unknown Christ of Hinduism' and of the other traditions, and indeed the unknown Christ within all creative transformations of individuals and societies. And, if we ask how this differs from simply saying that within all these different streams of human life there is a creative and re-creative response to the divine Reality, the answer of this kind of Christian inclusivism is that Christians are those, uniquely, who are able to identify the source of salvation because they have encountered that source as personally incarnate in Jesus Christ.

Both forms of inclusivism do however involve certain inner strains and certain awkward implications.[2] How are they to be combined with the traditional *Extra ecclesiam* dogma? The best known attempt is that of Karl Rahner, with his concept of the 'anonymous Christian'. Those who do not have an explicit Christian faith but who nevertheless seek, consciously or uncon-sciously, to do God's will can be regarded as, so to speak, honorary Christians – and this even though they do not so regard themselves and even though they may insist that they are not Christians but Muslims, Jews, Hindus, or whatever. Rahner's is a brave attempt to attain an inclusivist position which is in principle universal but which does not thereby renounce the old exclusivist dogma. But the question is whether in this new context the old dogma has not been so emptied of content as no longer to be worth affirming. When salvation is acknowledged to be taking place without any connection with the Christian Church or Gospel, in people who are living on the basis of quite other faiths, is it not a somewhat empty gesture to insist upon affixing a Christian label to them? Further, having thus labelled them, why persist in the aim of gathering all humankind into the Christian Church? Once it is accepted that salvation does not depend upon this, the conversion of the people of the other great world faiths to Christianity hardly seems the best way of spending one's energies.

The third possible answer to the question of the relation between salvation/liberation and the cumulative religious traditions can best be called pluralism. As a Christian position this can be seen as an acceptance of the further conclusion to which inclusivism points. If we accept that salvation/liberation is taking place within all the great religious traditions, why not frankly acknowledge that there is a plurality of saving human responses to the ultimate divine Reality? Pluralism, then, is the view that the transformation of human existence from self-centredness to Reality-centredness is taking place in different ways within the contexts of all the great religious traditions. There is not merely one way but a plurality of ways of salvation or liberation. In Christian theological terms, there is a plurality of divine revelations, making possible a plurality of forms of saving human response.

What however makes it difficult for Christians to move from inclusivism to pluralism, holding the majority of Christian theologians today in the inclusivist position despite its evident logical instability, is of course the traditional doctrine of the Incarnation, together with its protective envelope, the doctrine of the Trinity. For in its orthodox form, as classically expressed at the Councils of Nicaea and Chalcedon, the incarnational doctrine claims that Jesus was God incarnate, the Second Person of the Triune God living a human life. It is integral to this faith that there has been (and will be) no other divine incarnation. This makes Christianity unique in that it, alone among the religions of the world, was founded by God in person. Such a uniqueness would seem to demand Christian exclusivism – for must God not want all human beings to enter the way of salvation which he has provided for them? However, since such exclusivism seems so unrealistic in the light of our knowledge of the wider religious life of mankind, many theologians have moved to some form of inclusivism, but now feel unable to go further and follow the argument to its conclusion in the frank acceptance of pluralism. The break with traditional missionary attitudes and long-established ecclesiastical and liturgical language would, for many, be so great as to be prohibitive.

There is however the possibility of an acceptable Christian route to religious pluralism in work which has already been done, and which is being done, in the field of Christology with motivations quite other than to facilitate pluralism, and on grounds which are internal to the intellectual development of Christianity. For there is a decisive watershed between what might be called all-or-nothing Christologies and degree Christologies. The all-or-nothing principle is classically expressed in the Chalcedonian Definition, according to which Christ is 'to be acknowledged in Two Natures', 'Consubstantial with the Father according to his Deity, Consubstantial with us according to his Humanity'. Substance is an all-or-nothing notion, in that A either is or is not composed of the same substance, either has or does not have the same essential nature, as B. Using this all-or-nothing conceptuality Chalcedon attributed to Christ two complete natures, one divine and the other human, being in his divine nature of one substance with God the Father. Degree Christologies, on the other hand, apply the term 'incarnation' to the activity of God's Spirit or of God's grace in human lives, so that the divine will is done on earth. This kind of reinterpretation has been represented in recent years by, for example, the 'paradox of grace' Christology of Donald Baillie (in *God Was in Christ*, 1948) and the 'inspiration Christology' of Geoffrey Lampe (in *God as Spirit*, 1977). In so far as a human being is open and responsive to God, so that God is able to act in and through that individual, we can speak of the embodiment in human life of God's redemptive activity. And in Jesus this 'paradox of grace' – the paradox expressed by St Paul when he wrote 'it was not I, but the grace of God which is in me' (1 Corinthians 15:10), – or the inspiration of God's Spirit, occurred to a startling extent. The paradox, or the inspiration, are not however confined to the life of Jesus; they are found, in varying degrees, in all free human response to God. Christologies of the same broad family occur in the work of Norman Pittenger (*The Word Incarnate*, 1957), John Knox (*The Humanity and Divinity of Christ*, 1967), and earlier in John Baillie (*The Place of Jesus Christ in Modern Christianity*, 1929), and more recently in the authors of *The Myth of God Incarnate* (1977).

These modern degree Christologies were not in fact for the most part developed in order to facilitate a Christian acceptance of religious pluralism. They were developed as alternatives to the old substance Christology, in which so many difficulties, both historical and philosophical, had become apparent. They claim to be compatible with the teachings of Jesus and of the very early Church, and to avoid the intractable problem, generated by a substance Christology, of the relation between Jesus's two natures. But, as an unintended consequence, degree Christologies open up the possibility of seeing God's activity in Jesus as being of the same kind as God's activity in other great human mediators of the divine. The traditional Christian claim to the unique superiority of Christ and of the Christian tradition is not of course precluded by a degree Christology; for it may be argued (as it was, for example, by both Baillie and Lampe) that Christ was the *supreme* instance of the paradox of grace or of the inspiration of the Spirit, so that Christianity is still assumed to be the *best* context of salvation/liberation. But, whereas, starting from the substance Christology, the unique superiority of Christ and the Christian Church are guaranteed *a priori*, starting from a degree Christology they have to be established by historical evidence. Whether this can in fact be done is, clearly, an open question. It would indeed be an uphill task today to establish that we know enough about the inner and outer life of the historical Jesus, and of the other founders of great religious traditions, to be able to make any such claim; and perhaps an even more uphill task to establish from the morally ambiguous histories of each of the great traditions, complex mixtures of good and evil as each has been, that one's own tradition stands out as manifestly superior to all others.

I think, then, that a path exists along which Christians can, if they feel so drawn, move to an acceptance of religious pluralism. Stated philosophically such a pluralism is the view that the great world faiths embody different perceptions and conceptions of, and correspondingly different responses to, the Real or the Ultimate from within the major variant cultural ways of being human; and that within each of them the transformation of human existence from self-centredness to Reality-centredness is manifestly taking place – and taking place, so far as human observation can tell, to much the same extent. Thus the great religious traditions are to be regarded as alternative soteriological 'spaces' within which, or 'ways' along which, men and women can find salvation/liberation/enlightenment/fulfilment.

But how can such a view be arrived at? Are we not proposing a picture reminiscent of the ancient allegory of the blind men and the elephant, in which each runs his hands over a different part of the animal, and identifies it differently, a leg as a tree, the trunk as a snake, the tail as a rope, and so on? Clearly, in the story the situation is being described from the point of view of someone who can observe both elephant and blind men. But where is the vantage-point from which one can observe both the divine Reality and the different limited human standpoints from which that Reality is being variously perceived? The advocate of the pluralist understanding cannot pretend to any such cosmic vision. How then does he profess to know that the situation is indeed as he depicts it? The answer is that he does not profess to *know* this, if by knowledge we mean infallible cognition. Nor indeed can anyone else properly claim to have knowledge, in this sense, of either the exclusivist or the inclusivist picture. All of them are, strictly speaking, hypotheses. The pluralist hypothesis is arrived at inductively. One starts from the fact that many human beings experience life in relation to a limitlessly greater transcendent Reality – whether the direction of transcendence be beyond our present existence or within its hidden depths. In theory such religious experience is capable of a purely naturalistic analysis which does not involve reference to any reality other than the human and the natural. But to participate by faith in one of the actual streams of religious experience – in my case, the Christian stream – is to participate in it as an experience of transcendent Reality. I think that there is in fact a good argument for the rationality of trusting one's own religious experience, together with that of the larger tradition within which it occurs, so as both to believe and to live on the basis of it; but I cannot develop that argument here.[3] Treating one's own form of religious experience, then, as veridical – as an experience (however dim, like 'seeing through a glass, darkly') of transcendent divine Reality – one then has to take account of the fact that there are other great streams of religious experience which take different forms, are shaped by different conceptualities, and embodied in different institutions, art forms, and life-styles. In other words, besides one's own religion, sustained by its distinctive form of religious experience, there are also other religions, through each of which flows the life blood of a different form of religious experience. What account is one to give of this plurality?

At this point the three answers that we discussed above become available again: exclusivism, inclusivism and pluralism. The exclusivist answer is that only one's own form of religious experience is an authentic contact with the Transcendent, other forms being delusory: the naturalistic interpretation applies to those other forms, but not to ours. This is a logically possible position; but clearly it is painfully vulnerable to the charge of being entirely arbitrary. It thus serves the cause of general scepticism, as David Hume noted with regard to claims that the miracles of one's own religion are genuine whilst those of others are spurious.[4]

Moving to the inclusivist answer, this would suggest that religious experience in general does indeed constitute a contact with the Transcendent, but that this contact occurs in its purest and most salvifically effective form within one's own tradition, other forms having value to the varying extents to which they approximate to ours. This is a more viable position than the previous one, and less damaging to the claim that religion is not a human projection but a genuine human response to transcendent Reality. There is however a range of facts which do not fit easily into the inclusivist theory, namely the changed and elevated lives, moving from self-centredness towards Reality-centredness, within the other great religious traditions. Presumably there must be a strong correlation between the authenticity of the forms of religious experience and their spiritual and moral fruits. It would then follow from the inclusivist position that there should be a far higher incidence and quality of saintliness in one tradition – namely, that in which contact with the Transcendent occurs in 'its purest and most salvifically effective form' – than in the others. But this does not seem to be the case. There is of course no reliable census of saints! Nor indeed is the concept of a saint by any means clear and unproblematic; very different profiles of saintliness have operated at different times and in different places. But if we look for the transcendence of egoism and a recentring in God or in the transcendent Real, then I venture the proposition that, so far as human observation and historical memory can tell, this occurs to about the same extent within each of the great world traditions.

If this is so, it prompts us to go beyond inclusivism to a

pluralism which recognises a variety of human religious contexts within which salvation/liberation takes place.

But such a pluralistic hypothesis raises many questions. What is this divine Reality to which all the great traditions are said to be oriented? Can we really equate the personal Yahweh with the non-personal Brahman, Shiva with the Tao, the Holy Trinity with the Buddhist Trikāya, and all with one another? Indeed, do not the Eastern and Western faiths deal incommensurably with different problems?

As these questions indicate, we need a pluralistic theory which enables us to recognise and be fascinated by the manifold differences between the religious traditions, with their different conceptualisations, their different modes of religious experience, and their different forms of individual and social response to the divine. I should like in these final pages to suggest the ground plan of such a theory – a theory which is, I venture to think, fully compatible with the central themes of Cantwell Smith's thought.

Each of the great religious traditions affirms that in addition to the social and natural world of our ordinary human experience there is a limitlessly greater and higher Reality beyond or within us, in relation to which or to whom is our highest good. The ultimately real and the ultimately valuable are one, and to give oneself freely and totally to this One is our final salvation/ liberation/enlightenment/fulfilment. Further, each tradition is conscious that the divine Reality exceeds the reach of our earthly speech and thought. It cannot be encompassed in human concepts. It is infinite, eternal, limitlessly rich beyond the scope of our finite conceiving or experiencing. Let us then both avoid the particular names used within the particular traditions and yet use a term which is consonant with the faith of each of them – Ultimate Reality, or the Real.

Let us next adopt a distinction that is to be found in different forms and with different emphases within each of the great traditions, the distinction between the Real *an sich* (in him/her/it-self) and the Real as humanly experienced and thought. In Christian terms this is the distinction between God in God's infinite and eternal self-existent being, 'prior' to and independent of creation, and God as related to and known by us as creator, redeemer and sanctifier. In Hindu thought it is the distinction between *nirguṇa* Brahman, the Ultimate in itself, beyond all human categories, and *saguṇa* Brahman, the Ultimate as known to finite consciousness as a personal deity, Iśvara. In Taoist thought, 'The Tao that can be expressed is not the eternal Tao' (*Tao-Te Ching*, 1). There are also analogous distinctions in Jewish and Muslim mystical thought in which the Real *an sich* is called *en Soph* and *al Haqq*. In Mahāyāna Buddhism there is the distinction between the *dharmakāya*, the eternal cosmic Buddha-nature, which is also the infinite Void (*śūnyatā*), and on the other hand the realm of heavenly Buddha figures (*sambhogakāya*) and their incarnations in the earthly Buddhas (*nirmāṇakāya*). This varied family of distinctions suggests the perhaps daring thought that the Real *an sich* is one but is nevertheless capable of being humanly experienced in a variety of ways. This thought lies at the heart of the pluralistic hypothesis which I am suggesting.

The next point of which we need to take account is the creative part that thought, and the range of concepts in terms of which it functions, plays in the formation of conscious experience. It was above all Immanuel Kant who brought this realisation into the stream of modern reflection, and it has since been confirmed and amplified by innumerable studies, not only in general epistemology but also in cognitive psychology, in the sociology of knowledge, and in the philosophy of science. The central fact, of which the epistemology of religion also has to take account, is that our environment is not reflected in our consciousness in a simple and straightforward way, just as it is, independently of our perceiving it. At the physical level, out of the immense richness of structure and detail around us, only that minute selection that is relevant to our biological survival and flourishing affects our senses; and these inputs are interpreted in the mind/brain to produce our conscious experience of the familiar world in which we live. Its character as an environment within which we can learn to behave appropriately can be called its *meaning* for us. This all-important dimension of meaning, which begins at the physical level as the habitability of the material world, continues at the personal, or social, level of awareness as the moral significance of the situations of our life, and at the religious level as a consciousness of the ultimate meaning of each situation and of our situation as a whole in relation to the divine Reality. This latter consciousness is not however a general consciousness of the divine, but always takes specific forms; and, as in the case of the awareness of the physical and of the ethical meaning of our environment, such consciousness has an essential dispositional aspect. To experience in this way rather than in that involves being in a state of readiness to behave in a particular range of ways, namely that which is appropriate to our environment having the particular character that we perceive (or of course misperceive) it to have. Thus to be aware of the divine as 'the God and Father of our Lord Jesus Christ', in so far as this is the operative awareness which determines our dispositional state, is to live in the kind of way described by Jesus in his religious and moral teaching – in trust towards God and in love towards our neighbours.

How are these various specific forms of religious awareness formed? Our hypothesis is that they are formed by the presence of the divine Reality, this presence coming to consciousness in terms of the different sets of religious concepts and structures of religious meaning that operate within the different religious traditions of the world. If we look at the range of actual human religious experience and ask ourselves what basic concepts and what concrete images have operated in its genesis, I would suggest that we arrive at something like the following answer. There are, first, the two basic religious concepts which between them dominate the entire range of the forms of religious experience. One is the concept of Deity, or God, i.e. the Real as personal; and the other is the concept of the Absolute, i.e. the Real as non-personal. (The term 'Absolute' is by no means ideal for the purpose, but is perhaps the nearest that we have.) We do not however, in actual religious experience, encounter either Deity in general or the Absolute in general, but always in specific forms. In Kantian language, each general concept is schematised, or made concrete. In Kant's own analysis of sense-experience the schematisation of the basic categories is in terms of time; but religious experience occurs at a much higher level of meaning, presupposing and going beyond physical meaning and involving much more complex and variable modes of dispositional response. Schematisation or concretisation here is in terms of 'filled' human time, or history, as diversified into the different cultures and civilisations of the earth. For there are different concrete ways of being human and of participating in human history, and within these different ways the presence of the divine Reality is experienced in characteristically different ways.

To take the concept of God first, this becomes concrete as the range of specific deities to which the history of religion bears witness. Thus the Real as personal is known in the Christian tradition as God the Father; in Judaism as Adonai; in Islam as Allah, the Qur'ānic Revealer; in the Indian traditions as Shiva, or Vishnu, or Paramātmā, and under the many other lesser images of deity which in different regions of India concretise different aspects of the divine nature. This range of personal deities who are the foci of worship within the theistic traditions constitutes the range of the divine *personae* in relation to mankind. Each *persona*, in his or her historical concreteness, lives within the corporate experience of a particular faith-community. Thus the Yahweh *persona* exists and has developed in interaction with the Jewish people. He is a part of their history, and they are a part of his; and he cannot be extracted from this historical context. Shiva, on the other hand, is a quite different divine *persona*, existing in the experience of hundreds of millions of people in the Shaivite stream of Indian religious life. These two *personae*, Yahweh and Shiva, live within different worlds of faith, partly creating and partly created by the features of different human cultures, being responded to in different patterns of life, and being integral to different strands of historical experience. Within each of these worlds of faith great numbers of people find the ultimate meaning of their existence, and are carried through the crises of life and death; and within this process many are, in varying degrees, challenged and empowered to move forward on the way of salvation/liberation from self-centredness to Reality-centredness. From the pluralist point of view Yahweh and Shiva are not rival gods, or rival claimants to be the one and only God, but rather two different concrete historical *personae* in terms of which the ultimate divine Reality is present and responded to by different large historical communities within different strands of the human story.

This conception of divine *personae*, constituting (in Kantian language) different divine phenomena in terms of which the one divine noumenon is humanly experienced, enables us to acknowledge the degree of truth within the various projection theories of religion from Feuerbach through Freud to the present day. An element of human projection colours our mental images of God, accounting for their anthropomorphic features – for example, as male or female. But human projection does not – on this view – bring God into existence; rather it affects the ways in which the independently existing divine Reality is experienced.

Does this epistemological pattern of the schematisation of a basic religious concept into a range of particular correlates of religious experience apply also to the non-theistic traditions? I suggest that it does. Here the general concept, the Absolute, is schematised in actual religious experience to form the range of divine *impersonae* – Brahman, the Dharma, the Tao, *nirvāṇa*, *śūnyatā*, and so on – which are experienced within the Eastern traditions. The structure of these *impersonae* is however importantly different from that of the *personae*. A divine *persona* is concrete, implicitly finite, sometimes visualisable and even capable of being pictured. A divine *impersona*, on the other hand, is not a 'thing' in contrast to a person. It is the infinite being–consciousness–bliss (*saccidānanda*) of Brahman; or the beginningless and endless process of cosmic change (*pratītya samutpāda*) of Buddhist teaching; or again the ineffable 'further shore' of *nirvāṇa*, or the eternal Buddha-nature (*dharmakāya*); or the ultimate Emptiness (*śūnyatā*) which is also the fullness or suchness of the world; or the eternal principle of the Tao. It is thus not so much an entity as a field of spiritual force, or the ultimate reality of everything, that which gives final meaning and joy. These non-personal conceptions of the Ultimate inform modes of consciousness varying from the advaitic experience of becoming one with the Infinite, to the Zen experience of finding a total reality in the present concrete moment of existence in the ordinary world. And according to the pluralistic hypothesis these different modes of experience constitute different experiences of the Real as non- or trans-personal. As in the case of the divine *personae*, they are formed by different religious conceptualities which have developed in interaction with different spiritual disciplines and methods of meditation. The evidence that a range of *impersonae* of the one Ultimate Reality are involved in the non-theistic forms of religious experience, rather than the direct unmediated awareness of Reality itself, consists precisely in the differences between the experiences reported within the different traditions. How is it that a 'direct experience' of the Real can take such different forms? One could of course at this point revert to the exclusivism or the inclusivisim whose limitations we have already noted. But the pluralist answer will be that even the most advanced form of mystical experience, as an experience undergone by an embodied consciousness whose mind/brain has been conditioned by a particular religious tradition, must be affected by the conceptual framework and spiritual training provided by that tradition, and accordingly takes these different forms. In other words the Real is experienced not *an sich*, but in terms of the various non-personal images or concepts that have been generated at the interface between the Real and different patterns of human consciousness.

These many different perceptions of the Real, both theistic and non-theistic, can only establish themselves as authentic by their soteriological efficacy. The great world traditions have in fact all proved to be realms within which or routes along which people are enabled to advance in the transition from self-centredness to Reality-centredness. And, since they reveal the Real in such different lights, we must conclude that they are independently valid. Accordingly, by attending to other traditions than one's own one may become aware of other aspects or dimensions of the Real, and of other possibilities of response to the Real, which had not been made effectively available by one's own tradition. Thus a mutual mission of the sharing of experiences and insights can proceed through the growing network of inter-faith dialogue and the interactions of the faith-communities. Such mutual mission does not aim at conversion – although occasionally individual conversions, in all directions, will continue to occur – but at mutual enrichment and at co-operation in face of the urgent problems of human survival in a just and sustainable world society.

There are many topics which I have not had space to take up in this chapter. I have spoken of 'the great world traditions'; but what about the other smaller ones, including the many new religious movements which are springing up around us today? And what about the great secular faiths of Marxism and Maoism and humanism? Again, I have spoken of salvation/liberation as the transformation of human existence from self-centredness to Reality-centredness; but what about the social and political dimensions of this transformation? These are among the many important questions which any complete philosophy of religious pluralism must answer. But I hope that in this paper I may have said enough to indicate the possible fruitfulness of this general standpoint, a standpoint to which Wilfred Cantwell Smith's work has contributed so centrally and so notably.

NOTES

1. *Redemptor Hominis*, Vatican Polyglot Press trs. (London: Catholic Truth Society, 1979) para. 14.
2. For a further discussion of these strains, see pp. 52–3 below.
3. See Michael Goulder and John Hick, *Why Believe in God?* (London: SCM Press, 1983).
4. David Hume, *An Enquiry Concerning Human Understanding*, x. ii. 95. Para. 95.

4 Religious Pluralism and Absolute Claims*

The topic that I am going to pursue under this title is that of the absolute claims made by one religion over against others. Such a claim might be concerned with knowing and teaching the truth or with offering the final good of salvation/liberation. I suggest that in fact the truth-claim and the salvation-claim cohere closely together and should be treated as a single package. The valuable contents of this package, the goods conveyed, consist in salvation or liberation; and the packaging and labelling, with the identifying of the sender and the directing of the package to the recipient, are provided by the doctrine. Thus doctrines are secondary, and yet essential to the vital matter of receiving salvation, somewhat as packaging and labelling are secondary and yet essential to transmitting the contents of a parcel.

What then is an absolute claim when made on behalf of such a religious package? In this context the term 'absolute' is not, I think, being used as a precision instrument. Its operative meanings are revealed in its uses, which are in fact various. In one sense the absoluteness of, say, Christianity means the salvific sufficiency of its gospel and its way for Christians – that is, for those whose religious life is determined by that gospel and way. In this sense the absoluteness of Christianity is compatible with the absoluteness of Islam, or again of Hinduism, or Buddhism or Judaism, salvifically sufficient as these different messages and ways are for those who have been spiritually formed by them. But, since 'absolute' so strongly suggests uniqueness, and the impossibility of being surpassed or even equalled, it seems inappropriate to apply it to this pluralistic conception. And in fact this plural sense is the polar opposite of the religious absolutism that I want

* Reprinted, with permission, from *Religious Pluralism*, vol. 5 of the Boston University Studies in Philosophy and Religion (Notre Dame, Ind.: University of Notre Dame Press, 1984).

to discuss here. Let me approach it, however, through this opposite, namely religious pluralism.

By this I mean the view that the great world faiths embody different perceptions and conceptions of, and correspondingly different responses to, the Real or the Ultimate from within the major variant cultural ways of being human; and that within each of them the transformation of human existence from self-centredness to Reality-centredness is manifestly taking place – and taking place, so far as human observation can tell, to much the same extent. Thus the great religious traditions are to be regarded as alternative soteriological 'spaces' within which, or 'ways' along which, men and women can find salvation/liberation/fulfilment.

From this point of view the proper understanding of one's own religious faith and commitment in comparison with others' can be well expressed by adapting a phrase of Rosemary Reuther's. She speaks of her own commitment as a Roman Catholic, rather than as some other kind of Christian, as a matter of 'ecclesial ethnicity' rather than as involving a judgement that her church is superior to others.[1] Extending the idea, we may say that one's being a Muslim, or a Christian, or a Hindu, or whatever, is normally a matter of 'religious ethnicity'. That is to say, Christianity, or Buddhism, or Islam, or whatever, is the religious community into which one was born, into whose norms and insights one has been inducted, and within which (usually at least) one can therefore most satisfactorily live and grow. There are of course spiritual immigrants; but they are very few in comparison with the vast populations through which each religious tradition is transmitted from generation to generation. And having been born into, say, the Christian religious world one does not have to be able to prove (even to one's own satisfaction) that it is superior to the other religious worlds in order for it to be right and proper for one to be wholeheartedly a Christian. Realistically viewed, one's religious commitment is usually a matter of 'religious ethnicity' rather than of deliberate comparative judgement and choice.

But nevertheless each of the great traditions has long since developed a self-understanding which at some point jars, or even positively clashes, with this conception of religious pluralism.

Thus in the Hindu tradition one believes that one has access to the *sanātana Dharma*, the eternal truth, incarnated in human language in the Vedas. There is a general tolerance of other ways, often however combined with the assumption that sooner or later everyone in his or her own time – and if not in the present life then in another – will come to the fullness of the Vedic understanding. Further, in advaitic philosophy it is often held that the theistic forms of religion represent a less advanced awareness of the ultimate Reality. Thus 'Hinduism' is conscious, at least in many of its adherents, of its unique superiority among the religious movements of the world; and such a consciousness does not naturally encourage a genuine acceptance of religious pluralism.

In the Hebrew tradition it is held that the Jews are God's 'chosen people', partners in a special covenant, so that they may be God's means of revelation to all mankind. Thus, whilst to be a Jew has often involved special burdens and sufferings, sometimes of the most extreme and appalling kind, yet to be a Jew is also, from the Jewish point of view, to stand in an unique relationship to God. This does not lead to any general intolerance of other religions, nor to a feeling that their adherents must be converted to Judaism; but it does induce a sense of the privilege of having been born a Jew. However, religious pluralism implies that those who are on the other great ways of salvation are no less God's chosen people, although with different vocations; and a genuine acceptance of this is not naturally encouraged by the traditional Judaic self-understanding.

In the Buddhist tradition it is held that the true appreciation of our human situation occurs most clearly and effectively in the teachings of Gautama Buddha; and that any doctrine which denies the ceaselessly changing and insubstantial character of human life, or the possibility of attaining to the 'further shore' of *nirvāṇa*, is not conducive to liberation from the pervasive unsatisfactoriness of ordinary human existence. The Dharma is the full and saving truth, uniquely clear, effective and final among the illuminations and revelations of the world. And, again, such an assurance does not naturally encourage a full acceptance of religious pluralism.

In Islam there is the firm belief that Muhammad was 'the seal of the prophets' and that through the Qur'ān God has revealed to mankind the true religion, taking up into itself and fulfilling all previous revelations. Thus, whilst a Muslim should give friendly recognition to those within the other Abrahamic faiths and may even, in some interpretations, extend the Qur'ānic concept of the People of the Book to include those who encounter the divine through the Hindu, Buddhist, Confucian and Taoist as well as Jewish and Christian scriptures, yet he or she will retain a strong sense of the unique status of the Qur'ānic revelation. Here is God's final, decisive and commanding word which all must heed and obey. And such a conviction, again, does not naturally encourage a full and unqualified acceptance of religious pluralism.

And in the Christian tradition there is a powerful inbuilt basis for the sense of the unique superiority of the Christian faith in the doctrine that Jesus Christ, the founder and focus of the religion, was God himself – or more precisely, the Second Person of the divine Trinity – in human form. Given this basic dogma, it has been a natural historical consequence for Christians to see theirs as the one and only true religion, founded by God in person and the locus of God's unique saving act; with the corollary that all the other supposed ways to the Real are human constructions, not to be compared with that which God has personally provided. From this has flowed the missionary imperative (though considerably muted today within large sections of the Church) to convert all humanity to the acceptance of the Christian Gospel and to membership of the Church as the body of Christ's redeemed people.

Each of these great religious traditions, then, assumes in one way or another its own unique superiority. Psychologically, this may well only be an instance of the corporate self-respect that characterises any viable human group. The nearest parallel is national pride. What American would wish to be other than American, or what Chinese person would wish to be other than Chinese, or Nigerian other than Nigerian, or Briton other than British, or French man or woman other than French? And do not most people likewise take it unthinkingly for granted that their own mother tongue is the natural form of human speech, and that their own culture – with its familiar food, manners, art forms, and family structures, its pervasive presuppositions and atmosphere – represents the normative way of being human; so that they find it hard to see foreign ways of life as other than peculiar and, when strikingly different from their own, either laughable or bizarre. The other side of this natural parochialism, however, is that we are what we are, and are poor creatures if we do not take some satisfaction and pride in our own ethnic or national or cultural identity, however critical we may also be of some of its particular manifestations. Further, it is largely this residual tribalism that prompts us to work and sacrifice for the good of our community. And the same principle will naturally produce a corporate pride in any religious group of which we are members – both the immediate local community and the vast historical tradition which gives the latter its character and imparts to it its aura of sacredness. For we have – in most cases – been formed from infancy by our tradition, absorbing its values and presuppositions. It has become as much a part of us as our nationality, our language and our culture; and alien religious traditions can seem as peculiar or comic or bizarre as can foreign names or customs or foods.

Psychologically, then, the sense of the unique superiority of one's own religious tradition may be simply a natural form of pride in and ingrained preference for one's own familiar group and its ways. And thus far it is to be accepted and taken into account as an inevitable feature of human life; though it must not be allowed to inhibit the spiritual travel which has been called the imaginative 'passing-over' into another religious world and then coming back with new insight to one's own.[2]

But natural pride, despite its positive contribution to human life, becomes harmful when it is elevated to the level of absolute truth and built into the belief system of a religious community. This happens when its sense of its own validity and worth is expressed in doctrines implying an exclusive or a decisively superior access to the truth or the power to save. A natural human tribal preference thereby receives the stamp of divine approval or the aura of a privileged ralationship to the Divine. The resulting sense of a special status has in turn, in some cases, either spontaneously motivated or been manipulated to motivate policies of persecution, coercion, repression, conquest and exploitation, or a sense that others cannot be left to follow their own faith or insight but must be converted to one's own gospel. It is at this point, at which the sense of the superiority of one's own tradition is enshrined in formal doctrines, as an essential article of faith, that the idea of religious pluralism is felt as a challenge and may be resisted as a threat. It is also at this point however that the acceptance of religious pluralism can lead to creative doctrinal development.

It is for the adherents of each of the great traditions to look critically at their own dogmas in the light of their new experience within a religiously plural world. As a Christian I shall therefore direct my attention to Christian absolutism. In the past this has taken powerful forms, with immense human consequences, in the Roman Catholic dogma *Extra ecclesiam nulla salus* (outside the church, no salvation) and its nineteenth-century Protestant missionary equivalent: outside Christianity, no salvation. The former was expressed, for example, in the affirmation of the Council of Florence (1438–45) that

> no one remaining outside the Catholic Church, not just pagans, but also Jews or heretics or schismatics, can become partakers of eternal life; but they will go to the 'everlasting fire which was prepared for the devil and his angels', unless before the end of life they are joined to the Church (Denzinger, *Enchiridion Symbolorum Definitionum et Declarationum de Rebus Fidei et Morum*, 29th edn, no. 714)

whilst the latter was expressed in a message of the Congress on World Mission at Chicago in 1960, declaring that

> in the days since the war, more than one billion souls have passed into eternity and more than half of these went to the torment of hell fire without even hearing of Jesus Christ, who He was, or why He died on the cross of Calvary.[3]

There are today some Roman Catholic traditionalists, pre-Vatican II in outlook, who adhere to the *Extra ecclesiam* dogma in its full logical rigour; and likewise there are some Protestant fundamentalists who practice the nineteenth-century missionary faith in an unqualified form. Indeed, if we look at the entire Catholic and Protestant worlds, and not only at the parts with which we tend to be most familiar, we must say that there are today large numbers and powerful groups of Christian absolutists. But nevertheless I think that historians of twentieth-century Christianity will see as the more striking fact the progressive decay of absolutism during this period within the more active and self-critical layers of the Christian mind. The clear trend of mainline Catholic and Protestant attitudes is away from the absolutism of the past. But it is easier for this to happen at the level of practice than at the level of theological theory. For there can be no doubt that traditional Christian belief, as expressed in the scriptures, the ecumenical creeds, and the major dogmatic pronouncements and confessions, has been understood as embodying an absolute claim for the Christian Gospel and the Christian way of salvation. According to this system of belief, the historical Jesus was God the Son, the Second Person of the divine Trinity, living a human life; and by his death on the cross he has atoned for human sin, so that by responding to him in genuine repentance and faith, and gratefully accepting the benefits of his sacrifice, we may be reconciled to God and so become part of Christ's Church and heirs of eternal life.

Probably the majority of Christian theologians today want to remain loyal to the heart, at least, of this traditional teaching, centring upon the unique significance of Christ as God incarnate and as the source of human salvation, whilst however at the same time renouncing the old Christian absolutism. And so it has become common to give the old doctrines a universal rather than a restrictive meaning. It is taught that the salvation won by Christ is available to all mankind; though whenever and wherever it occurs it has been made possible only by his atoning death. His sacrifice on the cross is thus the necessary condition of human salvation; but its benefits may nevertheless be enjoyed by people who know nothing of him, or even who consciously reject the Christian interpretation of his life and death. Again, the divine Logos which became personally incarnate within the Jewish stream of religious life as Jesus of Nazareth has also been at work within other streams of religious life, inspiring spiritual leaders and thus being actively present (though no doubt in varying degrees) in Hinduism, Buddhism, Islam, and so on. Consequently there may well be significant religious lessons which Christians can learn from the people of these other traditions.

But I want to suggest that these moves, whilst admirably ecumenical in intent, only amount to epicycles added to a fundamentally absolutist structure of theory in order to obscure its incompatibility with the observed facts. In analogy with the old Ptolemaic picture of the universe, with our earth at its centre, traditional Christian theology sees the religious universe as centred in the person of Christ and his Gospel. In the history of astronomy, when new observations of the movements of the planets seemed to conflict with the Ptolemaic scheme smaller circles were added to the theory, centring on the original circles, to complicate the projected planetary paths and bring them nearer to what was observed; and these epicycles enabled the old picture to be retained for a while longer. Analogously, the Ptolemaic theology, with Christianity at the centre, is now being complicated by epicycles of theory to make it more compatible with our observations of the other great world faiths.

Purely theoretically, these moves can succeed. Further epicycles can be added indefinitely, as required, and the abandonment of the old scheme thereby indefinitely postponed. The problem is one not of logical possibility but of psychological plausibility. Natural human candidness sooner or later finds it unprofitable, and even perhaps undignified, to go on investing intellectual energy in defence of a dogma which seems to clash with the facts. And so when a simpler and more realistic model emerges there is liable to be a paradigm-shift such as took place in the Copernican revolution from the earth-centred to the helio-centric conception of the universe. In the theology of religions a comparably simpler and more realistic model is today available in the theocentric or, better, Reality-centred, conception with its pluralistic implications. Here the religious universe centres upon the divine Reality; and Christianity is seen as one of a number of worlds of faith which circle around and reflect that Reality.

A wholehearted shift to religious pluralism would mean abandoning not only the older and cruder Ptolemaic theology but also the more sophisticated versions with their new epicycles. For to hold that divine grace reaches the other worlds of faith via our own (i.e. via the person and cross of Christ) would be like holding that the light of the sun can only fall upon the other planets by being first reflected from the earth. To take a different analogy, it is as though there were a life-saving medicine the true chemical name of which is Christ. This medicine is available in its pure form only under the brand name of Christianity. But there are other products which, unknown to their purveyors, also contain Christ, though diluted with other elements and marketed under other names. In these circumstances a knowledgeable pharmacist would always recommend Christianity if it is available. However, there may be places where it is not available; and there, for the time being at least, another product will serve as an adequate second-best. This, I would suggest, is essentially the theology of religions created by the currently favoured theological epicycles.

But, once these epicycles are seen for what they are, it is I think clear that a Christian acceptance of religious pluralism must involve the kind of rethinking of the doctrine of the Incarnation that has in fact been taking place during the last fifty years or so. Let me briefly illustrate this, first, from one of the most influential of recent Roman Catholic thinkers, Karl Rahner. Although questions were raised by traditionalists in Rome about his orthodoxy, Rahner's position as a Catholic theologian was never successfully challenged and he is widely regarded as a prime example of one who was faithful to his own tradition but who at the same time accepted a responsibility to reformulate its affirmations in ways which are relevant and intelligible to the modern world.

In his much discussed article 'Current Problems in Christ-ology',[4] Rahner says that the Chalcedonian Definition is not to be seen as ending Christological thinking. For

> The clearest formulations, the most sanctified formulas, the classical condensations of the centuries-long work of the Church in prayer, reflexion and struggle concerning God's mysteries: all these derive their life from the fact that they are not end but beginning, not goal but means, truths which open the way to the – ever greater – Truth.[5]

Further, the traditional two-natures formula has often led in the past to

> a conception, which undoubtedly dominates the popular mind (without of course reaching the stage of consciously formulated heresy), and which could be put rather as follows: 'When our Lord (=God) walked on earth with his disciples, still humble and unrecognized . . . .'[6]

As against what Rahner sees as this popular misconception – which is however barely distinguishable from the traditional Christian conception of incarnation – we must, he writes, recognise the genuine humanity of Christ, which entails that

> the 'human nature' of the Logos possesses a genuine, spontane-ous, free, spiritual, active centre, a human selfconsciousness, which as creaturely faces the eternal Word in a genuinely human attitude of adoration, obedience, a most radical sense of creaturehood.[7]

For otherwise Christ 'would only be the God who is active among us in human form, and not the true man who can be our Mediator with respect to God in genuine human freedom'.[8]

Accordingly Rahner suggests that we should see the Incarnation not as the unique exception to God's normal relationship to man but rather as the uniquely perfect instance of that relationship. For

> Christological considerations have led the way back to the more general doctrine of God's relation to the creature and allowed Christology to appear as the clearly unique 'specifically' distinct perfection of this relation.[9]

Accordingly, the relation of created spiritual beings to God 'reaches its absolute peak in the case of Christ'.[10] Indeed, Rahner suggests in a striking phrase, 'Christology may be studied as self-transcending anthropology, and anthropology as deficient Christology'.[11] Thus the Incarnation is not to be seen as a divine intervention which lies apart from God's creative work in human life, but as

> the *ontologically* (not merely 'morally', an afterthought) unambiguous goal of the movement of creation as a whole, in relation to which everything prior is merely a preparation of the scene. . . . Consequently it is not pure fantasy (though the attempt must be made with caution) to conceive of the 'evolution' of the world *towards Christ*, and to show how there is a gradual ascent which reaches a peak in him.[12]

Hence Rahner can even see the Incarnation as the supreme instance of the operation of divine grace. For is not grace

> the unfolding within human nature of the union of the human with Logos . . . and is therefore, and *arising thence*, something which can also be had in those who are not the ek-sistence of the Logos in time and history but who do belong to his necessary environment?[13]

And so Rahner is able to say,

> Suppose someone says: 'Jesus is the man whose life is one of

absolutely unique self-surrender to God.' He may very well have stated the truth about the very depths of what Christ really is, *provided* that he has understood (a) that this self-abandonment presupposes a communication of God to the man; (b) that an absolute self-surrender implies an absolute self-communication of God to the man, one which makes what is produced by it into the reality of the producer himself; and (c) that such an existential statement does not signify something 'mental', a fiction, but is in the most radical way a statement about being.[14]

In a later paper, Rahner develops this thought that human nature is essentially endowed with the possibility of self-transcendence, and that 'The incarnation of God is therefore the unique, *supreme*, case of the total actualization of human reality, which consists of the fact that man *is* in so far as he gives up himself.'[15] For

> God has taken on human nature, because it is essentially ready and adoptable, because it alone, in contrast to what is definable without transcendence, can exist in total dispossession of itself, and comes therein to the fulfilment of its own incomprehensible meaning.[16]

In other words, divine incarnation in human life is a general human possibility. As Rahner says, in the context of a discussion of Christology in relation to the idea of evolution,

> It seems to me that we should have no particular difficulty in representing the history of the world and of the spirit to ourselves as the history of a self-transcendence into the life of God – a self-transcendence which, in this its final and highest phase, is identical with an absolute self-communication of God expressing the same process but now looked at from God's side.[17]

Thus incarnation is the ultimate human possibility, and will constitute the eschatological human reality. But in this world it has only actually happened in one unique case: 'it is only in Jesus of Nazareth that one can dare to believe such a thing has happened and happens eternally'.[18]

Clearly one could pursue this line of thought further by understanding incarnation as a matter of degree. We should then say that, whenever and wherever the grace of God is effective in men and women, evoking self-giving love for God and neighbour, to that extent God has become incarnate within human history. Such an enlarging – or, from a traditional point of view, metaphoricalising – of the idea of divine incarnation would have important implications for the Christian theology of religions. For, whereas an unique and absolute incarnation defines an unique stream of salvation history, incarnation understood as taking place in many degrees of human openness to the divine has no such effect.

However, Rahner is bound to the Chalcedonian tradition, according to which incarnation is unique and absolute. In Chalcedonian thinking this uniqueness and absoluteness are necessitated by the concept of substance. One is or is not of the eternal and uncreated substance of God the Father; this cannot be a matter of degree; and among all human life only Jesus Christ has been of that divine substance. Thus against the prompting of his own insights – as it must seem to the outside observer – Rahner insists that although Jesus was genuinely human yet also 'This man . . . is God.'[19] And in support of the traditional paradox that Jesus was unambiguously human and yet unambiguously God he propounds the following argument:

only a *divine* Person can possess as its own a freedom really distinct from itself in such a way that this freedom does not cease to be truly free even with regard to the divine Person possessing it, while it continues to qualify this very Person as its ontological subject. For it is only in the case of God that it is conceivable at all that he himself can constitute something in a state of distinction from himself. This is precisely an attribute of his divinity as such and his intrinsic creativity: to be able, by himself and through his *own* act *as such*, to constitute something in being which by the very fact of its being radically dependent (because *wholly* constituted in being), also acquires autonomy, independent reality and truth (precisely because it is constituted in being by the one, unique *God*), and all this precisely with respect to the God who constitutes it in being.[20]

Here Rahner attempts to render the paradox acceptable by the assertion that God, being God ('This is precisely an attribute of his divinity as such'[21]), can bring it about that, as incarnate, God is both a free, autonomous finite human person, and yet at the same time the infinite creator of all things. But the tortuous complexity of his argument conceals the simple proposition that God, being God, can do anything, and therefore can become a genuinely free and independent human being whilst remaining God. This is merely, however, to reiterate the traditional dogma without doing anything either to recommend it or to render it intelligible. Rahner's faithfulness to his tradition, with its implied absolute claim, is reflected consistently in his own theology of religions. Here it is assumed, on the basis of tradition, that redemption is through Christ alone and that outside the Church there is no salvation; but devout and godly people within the other great world traditions are to be regarded as 'anonymous Christians'. This has been Rahner's distinctive contribution to the spinning of epicycles in aid of a basically Ptolemaic theology. Given his adherence to the Chalcedonian Christology – despite exciting new insights which seem to point beyond it – the doctrine of the anonymous Christian is as far as he is able to go towards the alternative vision of religious pluralism.

However, let us turn at this point to the work of recent Protestant theologians who have also been trying to do justice to the genuinely human Jesus perceived by the modern historical reading of the Gospel records. The work of some of the more adventurous among them points to a way of understanding God's activity in the 'Christ-event' which does not in principle preclude an acceptance of religious pluralism. These theologians have not generally been primarily concerned with the question of other religions; and in so far as they touch upon it most of them adhere to the traditional assumption of the unique superiority of Christianity. But it is an important feature of their work – even if one which was not always noticed by these authors themselves – that whereas the Chalcedonian Christology entailed the unique superiority of Christianity these modern Christologies do not. Logically, they leave the comparative assessment of the Christian and other traditions to be determined – if it can be determined – by historical observation and spiritual judgement. Thus the superiority of Christianity loses its status as an *a priori* dogma and becomes a claim that could only be established by adequate historical evidence.

I shall illustrate this development from the work of the Presbyterian Donald Baillie and the Anglican Geoffrey Lampe, though American scholars such as John Knox and Norman Pittenger, to cite just two, would have served my purpose equally well.

The late Donald Baillie's book *God Was in Christ* was described by Rudolf Bultmann as 'the most significant book of our time in the field of Christology'.[22] Not only the title but the entire tone of Baillie's book shows that his intention was wholly orthodox. He was not criticising the idea of divine incarnation in Jesus Christ, but was trying to make it intelligible to our twentieth century. He did so by understanding incarnation in terms of what he called the paradox of grace. This is the paradoxical fact that when we do God's will it is true both that we are acting freely and responsibly, and also that God, through supernatural grace, is acting in and through us. The paradox is summed up in St Paul's words, concerning his own labours, that 'it was not I, but the grace of God which is with me'.[23] As Baillie says, the essence of the paradox

lies in the conviction which a Christian man possesses, that every good thing in him, every good thing he does, is somehow not wrought by himself but by God. This is a highly paradoxical conviction, for in ascribing all to God it does not abrogate human personality nor disclaim personal responsibility. Never is human action more truly and fully personal, never does the agent feel more perfectly free, than in those moments of which he can say as a Christian that whatever good was in them was not his but God's.[24]

Baillie now uses this paradox of grace as the clue to the yet greater paradox of the Incarnation: that the life of Jesus was an authentically human life and yet that in and through that life God was at work on earth. Baillie says,

What I wish to suggest is that this paradox of grace points the way more clearly and makes a better approach than anything else in our experience to the mystery of the Incarnation itself; that this paradox in its fragmentary form in our own Christian lives is a reflection of that perfect union of God and man in the Incarnation on which our whole Christian life depends, and may therefore be our best clue to the understanding of it. In the New Testament we see the man in whom God was incarnate surpassing all other men in refusing to claim anything for Himself independently and ascribing all the goodness to God. We see Him also desiring to take up other men into His own close union with God, that they might be as He was. And if these men, entering in some small measure through Him into that union, experience the paradox of grace for themselves in fragmentary ways, and are constrained to say, 'It was not I but God', may not this be a clue to the understanding of that perfect life in which the paradox is complete and absolute, that life of Jesus which, being the perfection of humanity, is also, and even in a deeper and prior sense, the very life of God Himself? If the paradox is a reality in our poor imperfect lives at all, so far as there is any good in them, does not the same or a similar paradox, taken at the perfect and absolute pitch, appear as the mystery of the Incarnation?[25]

In other words the union of divine and human action, which occurs whenever God's grace works effectively in a man's or a woman's life, operated to an absolute extent in the life of Jesus.

Now Baillie's suggestion – which has its roots in the thought of St Augustine, and earlier in Origen, and in Theodore of Mopsuestia and others of the later Antiochene school – does have the advantage that it offers some degree of understanding of what it means to say that the life of Jesus was a fully divine as well as a fully human event. But of course, in making the idea of incarnation thus to some extent intelligible, Baillie discards the traditional Chalcedonian language of Jesus having two natures, one human and the other divine, and of his being in his divine nature of one substance with the Father. That was a way of expressing it which made sense within the philosophical world of the early Christian centuries but which has now become little more than a mysterious formula which is obediently repeated but no longer bears any intrinsic meaningfulness. Thus the kind of reinterpretation that Baillie offers should be seen as an attempt to bring the doctrine of the Incarnation to life in the modern mind, giving it meaning as a truth which connects with our human experience and which is at least to some extent intelligible in contemporary terms. For, whilst few people today (outside the ranks of rather traditional professional theologians) use the concept of 'substance', or find the idea of a person with two natures other than grotesque, all Christians have some experience and appreciation of the reality of divine grace operating in human life. Further, they can connect this reality with the extraordinary events of the New Testament.

The other recent Protestant theologian to whose work I should like to refer is the Anglican Geoffrey Lampe, who was Regius Professor of Divinity at Cambridge University until his death in 1980. I shall be referring in particular to this last book, *God as Spirit*. Lampe uses as his clue or 'model' for the understanding of Christ the activity within human life of the Holy Spirit, the Spirit of God. And 'the Spirit of God', he says, 'is to be understood, not as referring to a divine hypostasis distinct from God the Father and God the Son or Word, but as indicating God himself as active towards and in his human creation'.[26] Again, 'The Spirit of God is God disclosing himself as Spirit, that is to say, God creating and giving life to the spirit of man, inspiring him, renewing him, and making him whole.'[27] The principal activity in relation to humanity of God as Spirit is inspiration; and accordingly the Christology which Lampe presents is 'a Christology of inspiration'.[28] For

> the concept of the inspiration and indwelling of man by God as Spirit is particularly helpful in enabling us to speak of God's continuing creative relationship towards human persons and of his active presence in Jesus as the central and focal point within this relationship.[29]

Again, 'The use of this concept enables us to say that God indwelt and motivated the human spirit of Jesus in such a way that in him, uniquely, the relationship for which man is intended by his Creator was fully realized . . . .'[30]

Accordingly Lampe does not accept the traditional model of 'the incarnation of a pre-existent divine being, the Logos who is God the Son'.[31] For that model is bound up with the two complementary notions of the primal fall of humanity from righteousness to sin, and then God's intervention by coming to earth in the person of Jesus of Nazareth to redeem mankind by the sacrifice of his own life upon the cross. Instead, Lampe prefers to follow the early Greek-speaking Fathers of the Church, such as

Irenaeus, in thinking of a continuous on-going divine creation of humankind:

> Irenaeus speaks of the making of man according to God's image and likeness as a continuous creation. . . . Man gradually progresses until he attains the perfection of created humanity, which consists in likeness to the perfection of uncreated deity. . . . Man, according to Irenaeus, is first moulded by God's hands, then he receives the infusion of the soul, the life-principle, and finally through Christ he is given the life-giving Spirit that makes him God's son.[32]

Thus, 'the Spirit transforms man into that which he was not; yet this transformation is continuous with creation; it is the completion of creation'.[33] On this view, the Spirit of God has always been active within the human spirit, inspiring men and women to open themselves freely to the divine presence and to respond in their lives to the divine purpose. This continuous creative activity of God as Spirit means that 'God has always been incarnate in his human creatures, forming their spirits from within and revealing himself in and through them.'[34] We must accordingly 'speak of this continuum as a single creative and saving activity of God the Spirit towards, and within, the spirit of man, and of his presence in the person of Jesus as a particular moment within that continuous creativity'.[35] For 'a union of personal deity with human personality can only be a perfected form of inspiration.'[36]

I suggest that in relation to the question of religious pluralism the momentous consequence of this kind of reinterpretation of the doctrine of the Incarnation is that it no longer necessarily involves the claim to the unique superiority of Christianity which the more traditional understanding involved. For if one says, with the older Christian formulations, that the divine substance was present on earth once and once only, namely in Jesus Christ, it follows as a corollary that the Christian religion, and no other, was founded by God in person; and it certainly seems in turn to follow from this that God must want all human beings to accept Christianity as the religion which God has created for them. From this starting-point, all other religious traditions have to be regarded as in various ways preliminary or defective or inferior – which is of course the way in which the Church has in fact usually regarded them in the past. But if, with Baillie, we see in the life of Christ a supreme instance of that fusion of divine grace and creaturely freedom that occurs in all authentic human response and obedience to God, then the situation changes. For we are no longer speaking of an intersection of the divine and the human which only occurs in one unique case, but of an intersection which occurs, in many different ways and degrees, in all human openness and response to the divine initiative. There is now no difficulty in principle in acknowledging that the paradox of grace was also exemplified in other messengers of God or indeed, more broadly, in other human beings who are markedly Reality-centred rather than self-centred.

Of course Christians who feel impelled to claim superiority for their own tradition can still find a way to do so. For they can claim that the paradox of grace, which occurs whenever a human being freely responds to God, was more fully exemplified in the life of Christ than in any other life. This indeed appears to have been Baillie's own view. But it is important to note that, whilst this is still a claim to an unique superiority, yet the epistemological nature of the claim has changed. It is no longer an *a priori* dogma but now is, or ought to be, a historical judgement, subject to all the difficulties and uncertainties of such judgements. Lampe also, given his understanding of God's action in Christ as the supreme instance of divine inspiration, is still able to make an unique claim for this particular moment of divine activity. For 'this moment is', he says, 'the fulfilment of all the divine activity which preceded it, and . . . it determines the mode in which God the Spirit is experienced in all subsequent history'.[37] 'The evidence', he continues, 'that this claim is justified is the actual fact that Christians find in Christ their source of inspiration, they are attracted by him to reorient their lives towards faith in God and love towards their neighbours, and they see in him the pattern of this attitude of sonship and brotherhood.'[38] However, that for which Lampe claims this unique significance is not the historical Jesus himself, in isolation, about whom our information is often fragmentary and uncertain, but the 'Christ-event' as a whole. 'The Christ-event . . . for which we claim so central a place in the history of the divine self-disclosure to man includes all human thought inspired by God which has Jesus as its primary reference-point.'[39] In other words, the uniquely central inspiration-event is virtually Christianity itself as a historical tradition focused upon the person of Jesus Christ. Thus Lampe says that,

> If a saying in the Gospels, such as, for instance, one of the Beatitudes, touches the conscience and quickens the imagination of the reader, it does not matter greatly whether it was originally spoken by Jesus himself or by some unknown Christian prophet who shared 'the mind of Christ'. It is in either case a word of God communicated through a human mind. It is an utterance of man inspired by God the Spirit.[40]

Thus it is not vitally important whether the famous words of Christ in the Gospels were actually spoken by the Jesus of history:

> We value them because we find truth in them and gain inspiration from them, and we acknowledge Jesus to be uniquely significant because he is either their author or else the originator of the impulse which evoked them from the minds of others – from people whose debt to him was so great that they composed them in his name, as his own.[41]

Here again, as in the case of Donald Baillie's 'paradox of grace' theory, we see a separating in principle of Christology from the theology of religions. That is to say, the unique superiority of the Christian revelation no longer follows as a logical corollary from either Baillie's or Lampe's Christology. To see Jesus as exemplifying in a special degree what Baillie calls the paradox of grace, and what Lampe calls the inspiration of God the Spirit, is thus far to leave open the further question as to how this particular exemplification stands in relation to other exemplifications, such as those that lie at the basis of some of the other great world religions. Baillie believes that the realisation of the paradox of grace (or of divine inspiration) in the life of Jesus was unique because total and absolute. But the point that I want to stress is that this belief is no longer, in the light of either Baillie's or Lampe's Christology, a necessary inference from the nature of God's action in Jesus, but must instead be a judgement based upon historical evidence. And the main problematic question that arises, for any Christian who is familiar with the modern scholarly study of the New Testament, is whether we have a sufficiently complete knowledge of the historical Jesus to be able to affirm that his entire life was a perfect exemplification of the paradox of grace or of divine inspiration.

We saw that in Lampe's thought there is a shift from the historical Jesus to the Christian movement as a whole as the locus of the uniquely 'central and focal' revelatory event. But if we do not have enough historical information to attribute absolute religious value to the historical Jesus we have, I should think, too much historical information to be able to make such a judgement about Christianity as an historical phenomenon. To Lampe it was self-evident that Christianity is the central and decisive strand of human history. But, clearly, this is not self-evident to those whose spiritual life has been developed in a different religious environment and whose relationship to the Divine has been shaped by a different spirituality. At this point Lamp is left witnessing to an unargued presupposition.

It is thus an important feature of these modern Christologies that, without necessarily intending this, they can make it possible for Christians to think without basic inconsistency in terms of religious pluralism. And my plea is that we should have an integrated faith in which our Christology and our theology of religions cohere with one another.

NOTES

1. *Theologians in Transition*, ed. James M. Wall (New York: Crossroad, 1981) p. 163.
2. John S. Dunne, *The Way of All the Earth* (New York: Macmillan; and London: Collier Macmillan, 1972) p. ix.
3. *Facing the Unfinished Task: Messages Delivered at the Congress on World Mission*, ed. J. O. Percy (Grand Rapids, Mich.: Eerdman, 1961) p. 9.
4. Karl Rahner, *Theological Investigations*, vol. i, trs. Cornelius Ernst, 2nd edn (London: Darton, Longman and Todd, 1965) ch. 5.
5. Ibid., p. 149.
6. Ibid., p. 157.
7. Ibid., p. 158.
8. Ibid., p. 160.
9. Ibid., p. 163.
10. Ibid., p. 164.
11. Ibid., p. 164, n. 1.
12. Ibid., p. 165.
13. Ibid., pp. 199–200.
14. Ibid., p. 172.

15. Karl Rahner, *Theological Investigations*, vol. IV, trs. Kevin Smyth (London: Darton, Longman and Todd, 1966) p. 110.
16. Ibid.
17. Karl Rahner, *Theological Investigations*, vol. V, trs. Karl-H. Krugger (London: Darton, Longman and Todd, 1966) pp. 178–9.
18. Rahner, *Theological Investigations*, vol. IV, p. 111.
19. Rahner, *Theological Investigations*, vol. I, p. 173.
20. Ibid., p. 162.
21. Ibid.
22. Quoted by John Baillie in D. M. Baillie, *The Theology of the Sacraments* (New York: Charles Scribner's Sons, 1957) p. 35.
23. Corinthians 15:10.
24. D. M. Baillie, *God Was in Christ* (London: Faber and Faber; and New York: Charles Scribner's Sons, 1948) p. 114.
25. Ibid., pp. 117–18.
26. Geoffrey Lampe, *God as Spirit* (Oxford: Clarendon Press, 1977) p. 11.
27. Ibid., p. 61.
28. Ibid., p. 96.
29. Ibid., p. 34.
30. Ibid., p. 11.
31. Ibid., p. 14.
32. Ibid., p. 18.
33. Ibid.
34. Ibid., . 23.
35. Ibid., p. 100.
36. Ibid., p. 12.
37. Ibid., p. 100.
38. Ibid.
39. Ibid., p. 106.
40. Ibid.
41. Ibid., p. 107.

5   On Grading Religions*

The idea of grading religions and placing them in an order of merit is to some repugnant, as involving a pretence to a divine perspective, whilst to others it seems entirely natural and proper, at least to the extent of their confidently assessing their own religion more highly than all others. We shall have to consider precisely what it is that might be graded, and in what respects and by what criteria. But, if we think for a moment of the entire range of religious phenomena, no one is going to maintain that they are all on the same level of value or validity. Indeed the most significant religious figures, the founders and reformers of great traditions, have invariably been deeply critical of some of the religious ideas and practices around them. Thus Gautama rejected the idea of the eternal atman or soul, which was integral to the religious thought of India in his time; the great Hebrew prophets criticised mere outward observances and sacrifices, proclaiming that what the Lord requires is to 'let justice roll down like waters, and righteousness like an ever-flowing stream' (Amos 5:24); Jesus, in the same tradition, attacked the formalism and insincerity of some of the religious leaders of his own time who 'tithe mint and rue and every herb, and neglect justice and the love of God' (Luke 11:42); Muhammad rejected the polytheism of his contemporary Arabian society; Guru Nanak in India and Martin Luther in Europe attacked much in the accumulated traditions into which they were born; and so on. Thus some kind of assessing of religious phenomena seems to be a corollary of deep religious seriousness and openness to the divine.

And we lesser mortals, who follow in the footsteps of these great spirits, can see that within our own tradition, even without attempting comparison with others, different aspects have to be regarded as higher or lower, better or worse, even divine and demonic. It will be sufficient for the moment to make the point as

---

* Reprinted, with permission, from *Religious Studies*, vol. XVII (1982).

a Christian looking at his own tradition. Christianity, as the strand of history which began with the life of Jesus, is immensely varied. The beliefs held by Christians have ranged from the sublime to the ridiculous – from, for example the belief that God loves us human creatures as an ideal father loves his children, to the belief that, to quote the 1960 Chicago Congress on World Mission, 'in the years since the war, more than one billion souls have passed into eternity and more than half of these went to the torment of hell fire without even hearing of Jesus Christ, who he was, or why he died on the cross of Calvary'.[1] Again, Christian practice has ranged from the saintly to the demonic – from, for example, the marvellous self-giving compassionate love of St Francis of Assisi or Mother Teresa of Calcutta, to the hatred expressed in the Christian persecutions of the Jews through some fifteen centuries. Thus it is obvious to a Christian, even without looking beyond the borders of the Christian tradition, that religion is not necessarily or always good and that some kind of assessment of religious phenomena is in principle in order. And the examples that I have given could readily be paralleled by an adherent of any other of the great world faiths looking at his or her own strand of religious history. Each tradition has to distinguish between higher and lower within its own life. Is there not then at least a *prima facie* case, not only for grading within a given tradition, but also for grading traditions, according to the adequacy of their conceptions of the divine and the value of the forms of life which flow from those conceptions?

In response to this question I am going to restrict my discussion to four of the world's major religious movements, two of semitic and two of Indian origin: Christianity and Islam, Hinduism and Buddhism. This selection will, I hope, be narrow enough to prevent the discussion from being completely unmanageable and yet wide enough to allow for comparison within each group and between the two groups. It does, however, mean leaving out of account immense ranges of the religious life of humanity, including primitive, or primal, religion; the ancient religions of Asia and the Mediterranean world which were in place when the great world faiths emerged; much of the religious life of China; and all of the new religious movements originating in the nineteenth and twentieth centuries, including those that are springing up around us today. It also means leaving aside the whole vast and immensely important phenomenon of modern secularism, both in its humanist and in its Marxist forms. A complete discussion would of course have to include all these other areas. But the central issues will I think confront us sufficiently, and indeed inescapably, through the four traditions that I have selected.

Let us begin by noting the broad common pattern in virtue of which it makes sense to attempt a comparative study of religions. For unless they had something in common it would be impossible to compare them, still less to grade them on a common scale. They do however in fact, I suggest, exhibit a common structure, which is soteriological in the broad sense that it offers a transition from a radically unsatisfactory state to a limitlessly better one. They each speak in their different ways of the wrong or distorted or deluded character of present human existence in its ordinary unchanged condition. It is a 'fallen' life, lived in alienation from God, or it is caught in the illusion of *māyā*, or it is pervaded throughout by *dukkha*. But they also proclaim, as the basis of their gospel, that the Ultimate, the Real, the True, with which our present existence is out of joint, is good, or gracious, or is to be sought or responded to: the ultimately real is also the ultimately valuable. It is a limitlessly loving or merciful God; or it is the infinite being–consciousness–bliss of Brahman; or the ineffable 'further shore' of *nirvāṇa*; or *śūnyatā*, in whose emptiness of ego the world of time and change is found again as fullness of 'wondrous being'. And, completing the soteriological structure, they each offer their own way to the Real – through faith in response to divine grace; or through total submission to God; or through the spiritual discipline and maturing which leads to *moksha* or to Enlightenment. In each case, salvation/liberation consists in a new and limitlessly better quality of existence which comes about in the transition from self-centredness to Reality-centredness.

This soteriological structure is embodied in two kinds of religious phenomena, cognitive and practical. The cognitive core of a religious tradition consists, as to its content, in a (putative) experience of the Real and, as to its form, in a basic vision of reality. The form and the content, however, belong inextricably together. Thus Vedantic saints experience their oneness with the eternal Self; and the basic vision informing this experience sees reality as the eternal Brahman, within which are our many illusorily distinct selves. Gautama experienced a total transcendence of ego in the moment of *nirvāṇa*; the informing vision being of a beginningless and endless process of interdependent change in which consciousnesses trapped in a false ego-identity, with all its sorrows and anxieties, can find liberation in the egolessness of *nirvāṇa*. Jesus experienced a filial relationship with God as his heavenly Father; and the informing vision sees reality as consisting in the all-loving and all claiming personal Creator and the creation. Muhammad experienced the overwhelming call of Allah to proclaim the divine message on earth; and his informing vision was, again, of God the absolute creator and lord, omnipotent and yet merciful, and the creation. Around these basic visions of reality subsequent generations constructed intellectual systems – theologies and religious philosophies – which interpret the meaning of the vision in terms of the concepts and styles of thinking available within their own cultural situations.

The other aspect of religious existence consists in the ways of life, both individual and communal, ritual and ethical, which flow from these different conceptions of the universe. The way of life, in so far as it is actually realised, is appropriate to the vision of reality. If one believes that God is gracious and merciful, one may thereby be released from self-centred anxiety and enabled to imitate the divine love and compassion. If one believes that one is, in one's deepest being, identical with the infinite and eternal Brahman, one will seek to negate the present false ego and its distorting vision in order to attain that which both transcends and underlies it. If one believes that ultimate reality is the Buddha-nature, and that the aim of living is to become a Buddha, one will seek to enter into the egoless openness and infinite compassion of the Buddha. And so with other pictures of reality; each, when deeply accepted, renders appropriate a style of life, a way of being human, which is also a way to the ultimate end of the Kingdom of God, heaven, eternal life, *nirvāṇa*, Buddhahood, *moksha*. . . .

By what criteria, then, may we assess and grade these different visions of reality and their associated ways of life?

If we ask how most people in fact do this, the answer is fairly clear. How does the ordinary, not highly learned or reflective, Christian or Muslim, Buddhist or Hindu, assess the relative merits of the visions of reality presented by his/her own and other traditions? One normally simply assumes, as a manifest fact, that one's own familiar tradition represents 'the truth, the whole truth, and nothing but the truth', and assesses other traditions in accordance with their similarities with and differences from it.

Such a procedure is indeed almost inevitable. One has been spiritually formed by a certain tradition, with its gospel or dharma, its revelation or teaching, its founder or book, its creeds and myths, its supporting community and spiritual discipline; and all this constitutes the religious air that one breathes, the religious sustenance by which one lives, the inspiration of one's peak experiences. As Ernst Troeltsch said, writing from a Christian standpoint, 'We cannot live without a religion, yet the only religion that we can endure is Christianity, for Christianity has grown up with us and has become part of our very being'.[2] And parallel statements could be made from a Muslim, a Buddhist, or a Hindu point of view. And so naturally one makes one's own tradition the touchstone by which to judge others. For, in all our judging, assessing, accepting and rejecting, we can only start from where we are, using such degree of truth as we have (or believe that we have) as our stepping-stone to further truth. And so one begins by looking at the other religious traditions of the world through the appraising eyes of one's own tradition.

But there is an obvious consideration which should prevent one from stopping at this point. Let me put it from my own point of view as a Christian. Traditionally, Christianity has rejected or subordinated other traditions because of its own claim to an unique and final revelation. But suppose that I, who am a Christian, had instead been born to devout Buddhist parents in a Buddhist culture. In one sense, of course, this is an impossible supposition. It is meaningless to say, 'If I (who am an Englishman) had instead been born a Thai, or a Burmese, or a Sri Lankan or a Japanese', for that person would not then be the present *me*. The point has to be put differently. When *someone* is born to Buddhist parents in a Buddhist culture, that person is very likely to be a Buddhist, and to be related to the Real in ways made possible by Buddhist understanding and practice. He or she will think of the Real as the Dharma or as the Buddha or as *nirvāṇa* or as *śūnyatā* (for there are wide variations within the Buddhist world), and find his or her own way to reality inwardly in meditation and outwardly on the Noble Eightfold Path. And, having been formed within the Buddhist tradition, with its own modes of understanding and its own forms of spirituality, he will experience Buddhism as 'the way, the truth, and the life' and see other forms of religious existence as better or worse according as they approximate to the Dharma. Again, when someone is born to devout Muslim parents within an Islamic society, that person is very likely to be a Muslim and to form his or her relationship to the transcendent through the ideas and spirituality of Islam. Such a person will think of the Real as Allah the all-merciful, and will see the way of salvation as submission to the divine will as revealed in the Qur'ān, a submission which has been aptly characterised as 'giving the world back to God'. Internalising this vision as his or her own vision of reality, and participating in its incarnation in human life, the same person will naturally see Islam as 'the way, the truth and the life' and will judge other reported revelations by the standard set in the holy Qur'ān. And so also when someone is born to devout Hindu parents in India; or indeed within any other powerful tradition. In all these cases, in which one's spiritual being and outlook are effectively formed by a particular stream of religious life, one naturally perceives it from within as 'the way, the truth, and the life' and judges alternatives in its light. And so we have the familiar world-wide situation of people being formed by a particular vision, which functions as the standard by which they judge all others.

There is a complication to be added to this picture in the fact of conversion from one tradition to another. However, as between the great world faiths these are marginal. For example, after the century or so of intense Christian missionary activity in India prior to independence and partition in 1947, the Christian population of the entire sub-continent is about 2.4 per cent.[3] Although numbering millions, and being influential out of proportion to their number, the Christian percentage remains marginal to the vast teeming of life of India, Pakistan and Bangladesh. And if one could add together all the adherents and fellow-travellers of the Indian-inspired movements in the Christian West – Theosophy, Divine Light, Self-Realisation, Hare Krishna, Transcendental Meditation, and so on,[4] and also all the Western adherents of Islam – European Muslims, Black Muslims, and the like – the total, although considerable, would still be similarly marginal. The broad fact is that the great missionary faiths – Buddhism, Christianity and Islam – successfully propagated themselves in their early periods of expansion, and still do so among the peoples of the 'primal' religions, but have met with only marginal success in areas that were already within the orbit of another of the great developed world faiths. Thus, whilst conversions occur and will presumably always occur, they do not significantly affect the broad picture of the massive transmission of each tradition from generation to generation in ways which makes it authoritative to those formed within it.

We are left, then, with the conclusion that in the great majority of cases – I should guess well over 95 per cent – the tradition within which a religious person finds his or her relationship to the Real depends to a very great extent upon where and when that person is born. For normally, in the world as a whole, the faith that a person accepts is the only faith that has been effectively made available to him or her. We can refer to this manifest dependence of spiritual allegiance upon the circumstances of birth and upbringing as the genetic and environmental relativity of religious perception and commitment. And it is an extraordinary, and to some a disturbing, thought that one's basic religious vision, which has come to seem so obviously right and true, has been largely selected by factors entirely beyond one's control – by the accidents of birth. It is not that one cannot move from one stream of religious life to another, but that this is a rare occurrence, usually presupposing privileged educational opportunities; so that the great majority of human beings live throughout their lives within the tradition by which they were formed. In view of this situation, can one be unquestioningly confident that the religion which one happens to have inherited by birth is indeed normative and that all others are properly to be graded by their likeness or unlikeness to it? Certainly, it is possible that one particular religious tradition is uniquely normative, and that I happen to have had the good fortune to be born into it. And indeed, psychologically, it is very difficult not to assume precisely this. And yet the possibility must persistently recur to any intelligent person, who has taken note of the broad genetic and environmental relativity of the forms of religious commitment, that to assess the traditions of the world by the measure of one's own tradition may merely be to be behaving, predictably, in accordance with the conditioning of one's upbringing.

These considerations do not logically oblige anyone to look for other criteria for assessing religious phenomena than simply their congruence or lack of congruence with the features of one's own tradition. But they do I think make it difficult to be happy with what might be called genetic confessionalism as a deliberate view. And so the search for criteria becomes one in which any reflective religious person can properly take part. The project is further supported by the thought that the kind of criteria that we are seeking must have been operating, at least to some extent, in the first phase of those religious traditions which have a founder and which began as a departure from an existing situation. For we cannot attribute the original positive response to Gautama, or to Jesus, or to Muhammad to the conditioning of Buddhist or Christian or Muslim upbringing. The general religious backgrounds of ancient India and the ancient Middle East respectively were of course importantly relevant. But human discriminative capacities must also have been at work, operating in accordance with at least implicit criteria, in the initial response to these great religious figures; and the question is whether we can uncover these criteria. Presumably essentially the same principles have operated in subsequent generations in each person's assessment of the tradition to which he or she adheres as belief-worthy, revelatory, plausible, rightly claiming allegiance. For a Christian, or a Buddhist, or a Muslim, or a Hindu has somehow concluded that their inherited tradition represents 'the way, the truth, and the life' – either absolutely or at least so far as that particular individual is concerned. And this concluding must have involved implicit principles of judgement, principles which we now want to try to discern.

If we ask the very basic question why a religious vision of the universe should ever be plausible to human beings, we can only appeal to the evident fact that we are religious animals, with a basic tendency to think of and to experience the world in terms of a more ultimate reality than that of our ordinary everyday consciousness. And if we next ask why a variety of religious conceptions and visions have become plausible within different streams of human life, we have I think to draw upon the fact that the main cultures of the world have been sufficiently different to constitute different ways of being human – including the Chinese, the Indian, the African, the Semitic and the Graeco-Semitic ways. These different ways of being human have involved different ways of being religious. One should not exaggerate the differences; for it is noteworthy that, as each major tradition has developed, it has become internally pluralistic and has produced within itself all the main forms of religious existence. Thus, the religious life of India includes both monistic and theistic strands; and religious thought in the West includes much more than a simple monotheism. But still there are manifest differences between the Semitic and the Indian ways of being religious, and between either of these and, say, the Chinese or the African ways.

We know all too little about the factors which have gone to shape the ancient cultures of the earth; but we do know something about the origins of the major religious traditions which have formed within them. These modes of awareness of, and ways of living in relation to, the Divine or the Real come about through human mediators – outstanding individuals who have been extraordinarily open and responsive to the higher reality. The primary mediators are the founders of religious traditions, whilst secondary mediators continue and develop these traditions. Those whom we can identify as the great primary mediators – Gautama, Confucius, Moses, Jesus, Muhammad – have initiated streams of religious life that have lasted for many centuries and that have drawn into themselves hundreds of millions of people. (There are also lesser founders of new traditions or sub-traditions, such as Guru Nanak, Joseph Smith, Mary Baker Eddy, Baha'ullah, Annie Besant, Kimbangu, Mokichi Okada, and many others, whose movements presuppose and arise out of one or other of the existing traditions.) The primary mediators are personally present or remembered, as in the cases of Gautama, Confucius, Jesus and Muhammad, or are concealed as the anonymous authors of, for example, the Vedas, the Upanishads or the Pentateuch; and in these cases secondary mediators inevitably assume a proportionately more important role in the developing tradition.

Now when human beings respond to a religious figure, so that that person becomes, through their response, a *mediator* of the divine, what criteria are operating? One, surely is a moral criterion. Although detailed moral codes often differ widely from society to society, and meta-ethical theories are highly various and often incompatible, there does seem to be a universal capacity to distinguish (though always within the framework of certain assumptions) between benefiting and harming, and a tendency to bestow moral praise upon actions which benefit and blame upon those which harm others. Basically, the notion of a morally bad action is that of an action which is believed in some respect to harm some community or person; and the notion of a morally praiseworthy action is that of one which in some way either wards off harm to or promotes the welfare of the community or one or more of its members. Given this basic consensus, the varying beliefs and assumptions within which it operates produce the differences between the specific moral codes of different societies. (For example, the cannibal's belief that in eating the flesh of a dead enemy one is thereby taking into oneself certain of that person's qualities, clearly affects estimates of the kinds of actions that produce a benefit.) There are also importantly different assumptions concerning the diameter of the circle of human beings who properly count when assessing benefit and harm. An absolute egoist would attach moral significance only to what affects him or her; members of a primitive tribe commonly counted only fellow members; a nation state normally attributes greater value to its own citizens than to foreigners; whilst for the modern liberal moral outlook all human beings count, and count equally, as those who may be benefited or harmed by human actions.

Now when we encounter, whether directly or indirectly, one who claims or is claimed to be a mediator of the divine or of religious truth, we take note of the supposed mediator's moral character, and would be unable to accept that person as genuine if he or she seemed to us morally questionable. Let us take Jesus as an example. Here the mediator and the message form a whole, and it is to this whole that the Christian responds. The teaching is accepted partly because the mediator is accepted, and the mediator is accepted partly because the message is. It is the coherence of the two – a body of teaching about God, and about how men and women should live as God's children, together with a life lived in history on the basis of that teaching – that is so impressive. No one aspect of the teaching was in fact strictly new or peculiar to Jesus; but the living of that teaching in a historical personality has made a profound impression, haunting the moral imagination of millions ever since. But if Jesus had taught hatred, selfishness, greed, and the amassing of wealth by exploiting others, he would never have been regarded as a true 'son of God', revealing the divine to mankind. His teaching went far beyond the accepted morality of his hearers, but it went further in, so to speak, the same direction, rather than calling for a reversal in which evil was now to be called good and good evil. His followers would not have been able to recognise as having authority a body of teaching that sheerly contradicted their own present moral insight. And again the moral teaching, however sublime, would not have gripped them as it did if it had not been incarnated in

Jesus's own life. If Jesus had not lived in accordance with his own teaching, but had been seen by those who began to follow him to be selfish, cynical, deceitful, and unscrupulous, then the Jesus movement would never have developed as it did into the great world faith which we know as Christianity. The same is, I believe, true of each of the other great mediators of the divine to mankind. And so we can I think confidently identify the operation of an ethical criterion in the recognition of a mediator of the Divine or the Real.

A second element in our acceptance of someone as such a mediator is that he – for so far the major mediators have all been men – opens up a new, exciting and commanding vision of reality in terms of which people feel called to live. It may be theistic, so that as they begin to experience life in terms of it they become aware of living in God's gracious presence and under God's limitless claim. Or it may be a non-theistic vision; and as it becomes their own they feel called to transcend the empirical ego which obscures their true nature. The mediator is possessed by his own vision of reality, and experiences in terms of it; and in setting it before others he finds that he is launching a new spiritual movement. His vision must of course be capable of being plausible to his hearers; and this has always required a sufficient continuity between the new message and the basic assumptions of the culture in which both mediator and hearers participate. Thus Confucius was unmistakably Chinese, Gautama unmistakably Indian, Jesus and Muhammad unmistakably of the Semitic religious world; and we cannot realistically imagine, say, Christianity having begun in fifth-century-BC India and Buddhism in first-century-CE Palestine, or Islam as having originated in fifth-century-BC China and Confucianism in sixth-century-CE Arabia. Each presupposes a religio-cultural situation within which the mediator's message had a basic intelligibility and plausibility. Thus religious founders have to be children of their own time as well as, and indeed as a prerequisite of being, the creators of new traditions. But, given this condition, it is a major element in the emergence of a great mediator that he perceives and presents to suffering humanity a new vision of reality in which the divine is real and is at hand and in which there is therefore hope for a limitlessly better existence.

The third element in the power of the mediator to win acceptance for his message is an extension of the second, namely that the new vision of reality be able so to possess our minds and hearts as to exhibit a transforming power in our lives. For such a vision is not, to those who see through its lens, a mere theory or hypothesis; it is a fresh way of experiencing, into which they are swept up and by which they are carried forward into a new life. Thus, Gautama was so powerfully conscious, in his Enlightenment, of the way of liberation from the misery of self-centredness to the ego-free state of *nirvāṇa*, and so fully manifested this liberated state in his life and his teachings, that his influence has led many others to follow the same path. His mediation of the Real was authenticated by a transformation in the consciousness and behaviour of those who responded to his message. Again, Jesus, through the power of his own intense awareness of the present reality and demanding love of the Heavenly Father, drew others into that same awareness. And living in the assurance of God's love they were set free from self-concern to love one another; seeing the world as God's world (even though still in process of being rescued from the power of the devil) they could live confidently and without anxiety for the future. Again, Muhammad was so overwhelmingly aware of the power of divine self-revelation, setting forth the true pattern of life and claiming our absolute obedience, that his call to give the world back to God in free submission exploded in people's minds and spread within a century across nearly half the globe.

We have, then, three factors which can be discerned in the founding of religious traditions. First, the life of the mediator of the Divine or the Real was such that the ordinary moral sense of humanity could recognise him to be good rather than evil; and his ethical teaching was such that it could be recognised as showing, more fully than the common morality of the time, the demands of Reality for the living of human life. Second, he saw and offered a vision of Reality as ultimately good and such that a new and better existence is possible within or in relationship to it. And third, as people have taken the step of living in terms of this vision, they have in fact been transformed (whether suddenly or gradually) and so have received a first-hand assurance that Reality has indeed been mediated to them.

But after the initial impact of the original revelatory event the new vision, and its transformation of human life, became in each case diffused throughout a culture or family of cultures; whilst in the Hindu instance, with no individual founder, the developing tradition was always culturally incarnated. Thus, whether the basic vision originated suddenly or gradually, aspects of it have been major ingredients in the development of cultures, whilst other and more ultimately demanding aspects have effectively moulded the lives of only a relatively few individuals and small communities, though still haunting the majority as an unattained ideal.

Cultures exist in the lives of peoples and nations, sharing their fortunes amid the contingencies of history. Each religious culture has enjoyed its high periods of flourishing and creativity and has endured periods of stagnation and depression. But through all these ups and downs their distinctive visions have continued and lives have been in varying degrees transformed through their influence. Men and women have been uplifted, and have moved towards human fulfilment, continuously or spasmodically, quietly or dramatically, amidst all the political turmoil and moral and spiritual ambiguities of the different phases of history. At the same time, whilst the religious visions have in varying degrees transformed many living within them, others have used those traditions to validate their own acquisitiveness and lust for power. Thus each tradition, viewed as an historical reality spanning many centuries, is an unique mixture of good and evil, embodied in the lives of saints and sinners, sometimes forming liberating but more often oppressive social structures, giving birth both to human nobility and to human beastliness, to justice and injustice, to beauty and ugliness. Each is an unique historical totality, a spiritual mansion within which millions live, being formed by it from birth and contributing in some small measure to shape its continuing development from generation to generation.

Now our question is whether, and if so how, we can grade these vast religio-cultural totalities.

We have, I suggest, two tools with which we can try to measure and grade aspects at least of them. One is reason applied to their beliefs; and the other is conscience, or moral judgement, applied to the historical out-working of those beliefs. Let us first deploy the rational tool. Can we apply it to the basic religious experiences, and the visions of reality which inform them? It does not appear, first, that we can speak of the rationality or irrationality of an experience. It is not experiences, but people and their beliefs and reasonings, that are rational or irrational. The distinctive experiences of Gautama, Jesus, Muhammad, and the Hindu saints, which lie at the originating basis of Buddhism, Christianity, Islam and Hinduism, were not rational constructs; they were, putatively, encounters with reality. Each of these root experiences was overwhelmingly powerful, and could only be accepted as authentic by the person whose experience it was. The test of the veridical character of such an experience must thus be the test of the larger religious totality which has been built around it. And such a test can only be pragmatic: is this complex of religious experience, belief and behaviour soteriologically effective? Does it make possible the transformation of human existence from self-centredness to Reality-centredness? This is an empirical rather than a rational test. Nor does it appear, second, that we can speak of the rationality or irrationality of the visions of reality associated with those basic experiences. For they are linguistic pictures or maps of the universe, whose function is to enable us to find salvation/liberation, the limitlessly better quality of existence that the nature of reality is said to make possible. They accordingly test themselves by their success or failure in fulfilling this soteriological function. The final verification is thus eschatological. For a few the eschaton has already been realised in the present; but for the great majority its complete fulfilment lies in the future. In that future it may turn out that the root visions were maps of different possible universes, of which only one at most is actualised; or it may turn out that they were analogous to maps of the same world drawn in radically different projections, each method of projection distorting reality in a different fashion and yet enabling the traveller successfully to find his or her way. But it is clear that the character of the universe and our place within it will become known to us, if at all, by experience and observation, not by reasoning; and so it does not seem that the tool of reason can enable us to test and assess the different basic religious experiences and their associated visions of reality.

We have already noted however that around each basic vision subsequent generations of thinkers have built interpretative systems of thought, which are Christian or Muslim theologies and Hindu or Buddhist religious philosophies. Rational scrutiny of these systems is clearly in principle possible. We can try to assess such a system in respect of its internal consistency and its adequacy both to the particular form of experience on which it is based and to the data of human experience in general. The four major religions that we are considering have in fact produced a rich variety of theologies and philosophies, and within each tradition there is ample scope for argument as to which of these is most adequate to the basic vision or most successful in interpreting that vision to a new age. We can also compare the family of theories within a given tradition with that created within another tradition. I do not think, however, that such a comparison can lead to the conclusion that one set of theories intellectually outclasses the rest. Each family, of course, contains more impressive and less impressive members. But their best representatives seem to constitute intellectual achievements of the first rank. I doubt whether the great enduring systems of Thomas Aquinas, al-Ghazali, Shankara, and Buddhaghosha can realistically be graded in respect of their intellectual quality. They seem, broadly speaking, to be equally massive and powerful systematisations of different basic visions. Each system of course focuses its attention upon some aspects of human experience and knowledge whilst being relatively indifferent to others. Each accordingly accounts for some facts better than for others. But any grading of them in this respect has to fall back upon a grading of the basic visions which they articulate; and this, we have noted, cannot be achieved by any intellectual test. The test is whether these visions lead to the better, and ultimately the limitlessly better, quality of existence which they promise. And so I conclude, thus far, that we cannot grade the great world traditions by means of the tool of reason.

Let us then turn from the intellectual to the spiritual and moral fruits of a basic religious experience and vision. We need to look both at the ideal fruit, visible in the saints of a given tradition, and also at the ordinary life of millions of ordinary people as it takes place within the actual history of that tradition.

The transformations of human existence which the different major visions produce appear, as we see them described in their scriptures and embodied in the lives of their saints, to be equally radical in their nature and equally impressive in their outcomes. Each involves a voluntary renunciation of ego-centredness and a self-giving to, or self-losing in, the Real – a self-giving which brings acceptance, compassion, love for all humankind, or even for all life.

Thus the Christian gives himself or herself to God in Christ in a total renunciation of the self-centred ego and its concerns. The Christian can then say, with St Paul, 'it is no longer I who live, but Christ who lives in me' (Galatians 2:20). And in this new state, as part of the communal Body of Christ, the Church, the believer acts, ideally, in self-giving love toward all humankind. The two interlinked commands are to love God and to love one's neighbour – who is anyone with whom one has to do. For, 'if anyone says, "I love God", and hates his brother, he is a liar; for he who does not love his brother whom he has seen, cannot love God whom he has not seen' (I John 4:20). This ideal of self-giving love, whilst always part of the Christian tradition, has been particularly prominent within the modern period of liberal and democratic thought. Whereas in early and medieval Christianity the person recognised as a saint was often a solitary ascetic, practising fearsome austerities, today the ideal is that of the great servant of humanity, seen in the past in St Francis and exemplified in our own century by, for example, Albert Schweitzer or Mother Teresa.

The Muslim, too, totally submits to God, renouncing the self-centred ego and its concerns, and living as a servant of Allah. The Muslim is taught by the prophet Muhammad that 'All creatures of God are His family; and he is most beloved of God who loveth His creatures'.[5] The virtues of the good Muslim are described in the Qur'ān in characteristically concrete and earthly terms. A Muslim should be kind to all: 'Be kind to parents, and the near kinsman, and to orphans, and to the needy, and to the neighbour who is of kin, and to the neighbour who is a stranger, and to the companion at your side, and to the traveller, and to that your right hands own' (4:40). A Muslim should be humble, for 'The servants of the All-merciful are those who walk in the earth modestly and who, when the ignorant address them, say "Peace" ' (25:64); and forgiving: 'But if you pardon, and overlook, and if you forgive, surely God is All-forgiving' (64:14). A Muslim should be honest and trustworthy: 'And fill up the measure when you measure, and weigh with the straight balance' (17:37) (Arberry's translation). The ethical ideal of Islam is summed up in the words of the Prophet in his sermon on entering Medina; it is that of 'loving God with all their heart and loving one another in God' (Ibn Hisam, Sira II, 348).

The aim of the Buddhist, again, is finally to transcend the ego, with its desires and anxieties, and to enter the ego-free state of *nirvāṇa*. The way to this is the Noble Eightfold Path, which is both spiritual and ethical. It produces compassion (*karuna*) and loving-kindness (*metta*) for all mankind, and indeed for life in every form. The disciple of the Buddha is 'to pervade each of the four quarters of the horizon with a heart charged with love, with pity, with sympathy in joy, with equanimity'.[6] This universal love of the selfless person is embodied in the ideal of the Bodhisattva, who voluntarily renounces the bliss of *nirvāṇa* until all mankind had been brought to the same point. The universal unity of humanity is a basic Buddhist conviction.

When we turn to Hinduism we find that its only essence is that it has no essence; for the name is an umbrella term for most of the religious life of India over a period of three millennia. In this pluralistic religious universe different ways of liberation are recognised and on each way there are stages, so that what is appropriate at one stage may not be appropriate at another. In India's most influential scripture, the *Bhagavad Gita*,* two ways are set forth, both involving the ideal of universal love and compassion which had been introduced into the religious thought of India centuries earlier by the Buddha. One way, that of meditation, leads to union with the Ultimate as the non-personal Brahman. Of those who follow this path it is said that they are 'in all things equal-minded, taking pleasure in the weal of all contingent beings' (12.4). The other way is that of action in the world, but action without concern for the fruits of action, in communion with the Ultimate Person, who speaks in the *Gita* as Krishna. And to those who follow this path of devotion and selfless action the Lord says, 'Let a man feel hatred for no contingent being, let him be friendly, compassionate; let him be done with thoughts of "I" and "mine", the same in pleasure as in pain, long-suffering, content and ever-integrated, his purpose firm, his mind and soul steeped in ME' (12:13–14).

These are, in briefest cameo, the ideal ways of life which follow from the different root experiences and visions of reality around which the four traditions have grown. If every Christian and Muslim, every Hindu and Buddhist, fully incarnated their respective ideals, they would live in a basic acceptance and love of all their fellow human beings. For they would have turned away from the self-centredness which is the source of acquisitiveness, dishonesty, injustice and exploitation. A world which practised the common ethical ideal of these traditions would have realised human brotherhood on earth. But of course in fact the ideal has

* All quotations from *The Bhagavad Gita* are based on the translation by R. C. Zaehner (Oxford: Clarendon Press, 1969).

only been realised in any substantial way in the lives of comparatively rare individuals and small religious communities, and spasmodically and in varying degrees in much larger ranges of individuals. The actual histories of Hindu, Buddhist, Christian and Muslim societies include, as a prominent part of the story, violence and war, oppression, exploitation and slavery, deceit and dishonesty, ruthless cruelty and a selfish grasping for wealth and power. These traditions have all nurtured not only saints and leaders in righteousness who have given themselves for the welfare of their fellows, but also evil and demonic figures, leaders in aggression and aggrandisement, who have cruelly exploited and oppressed their fellows.

Amidst history's long and depressing catalogue of 'man's inhumanity to man', can any one of the great religio-cultural streams of life claim a relatively greater virtue and establish itself as ethically superior to the others? I want to suggest that it is entirely possible that there is an ethical ranking of religious civilisations, with one rightly appearing at the top of the list. But I also want to suggest that we are not in fact able to make the comparative assessment which might lead to such a result. Thus, if we consider the case, widely accepted within Western society, for the moral superiority of Christian civilisation over the Muslim, Hindu and Buddhist civilisations, we find that for each evil that the Christian can point to in one of the other streams of religious history there is an equally evident evil within his own; and that it is impossible realistically to weigh these often incommensurate evils against each other.

How are we to weigh the lethargy of many Eastern countries in relation to social and economic problems, so that they suffer from endemic poverty, against the West's ruthlessly competitive greed in the exploitation of the earth's resources – the Western capitalist rape of the planet at the expense of half the world and of all future generations? How are we to weigh the effect of Hindu and Buddhist 'otherworldliness' in retarding social, economic and technological progress against the use of the Christian Gospel to validate unjust social systems in Europe and South America, and to justify and perpetuate massive racial exploitation in South Africa? How are we to weigh the unjust caste-system of India against the unjust class-system and pervasive racism of much of the Christian West? How do we weigh the use of the sword in building great Muslim, Hindu and Buddhist empires against the use of the gun in building the great Christian empires? How do we weigh the aggressive Muslim incursion into Europe in the fourteenth century against the previous Christian incursion into the Middle East known as the Crusades? How do we weigh the hideous custom of the 'voluntary' burning of widows (*suttee*) in India against the equally hideous burning of 'witches' in Christian Europe and North America? How do we weigh the savage aspects of life in some Eastern and Middle Eastern countries – the bloody massacres at the time of the partition of India, the cutting off of a thief's hands under Islamic law – against the Christian persecution of the Jews throughout the ages and above all in our own century?

The fact is that each of these four strands of history exhibits its own distinctive mixture of virtues and vices. Each has a relatively good record in some respects but a bad record in others. Broadly speaking, for example, Christianity has done well in stimulating the creation of wealth and the goods which wealth can make possible, but is badly stained by a record of perennial violence and persecution; whilst Buddhism, in contrast, has been much more peaceful, never giving rise to wars of religion, but has often failed to combat poverty and social injustice. And comparable contrasts occur with any other pair. The resulting patterns are so different that it is, surely, impossible to sustain either the common Christian assumption, or the parallel Muslim, Hindu, or Buddhist assumption, that one's own strand of history is haloed with a discernible moral superiority.

But does not Christianity perhaps have a unique historical position as the tradition within which our modern conceptions of universal human equality and freedom have arisen, in the light of which we have been identifying the evils of the different traditions? These modern liberal ideas have indeed first emerged in the West; but they are essentially secular ideas, which have been and are as much opposed as supported within the Christian churches. Contemporary Marxist, humanist and feminist critiques of economic, racial and sexual oppression have become common currency in Western liberal thinking, and have evoked their echoes in liberation and black and feminist theologies. But it would be erroneous to conclude, from the fact that these ideas have affected Western Christianity first among the religions, that Christianity has a proprietary interest in them. Our contemporary Western liberal–democratic, politically, racially and

sexually liberated form of Christianity represents a creative
synthesis of the Christian tradition with secular liberalism; and
analogous syntheses are beginning to emerge within the other
traditions. When today we condemn slavery, the Inquisition and,
say, the nineteenth-century persecutions of the Jews, we do so
from the modern liberal standpoint, not from that of the Christian
populations which engaged in those activities. And it is through
its participation in this same modern liberal standpoint that India
has officially renounced the caste-system, that polygamy is dying
out and women are seeking their liberation in modern Muslim
countries, and that Shinto and Buddhist Japan has become one of
the world's most efficient industrial powers.

Let me now offer my conclusions.

First, religious phenomena – patterns of behaviour, experiences, beliefs, myths, theologies, cultic acts, liturgies, scriptures,
and so forth – can in principle be assessed and graded; and the
basic criterion is the extent to which they promote or hinder the
great religious aim of salvation/liberation. And by salvation or
liberation I suggest that we should mean the realisation of that
limitlessly better quality of human existence which comes about
in the transition from self-centredness to Reality-centredness.

But, second, the ways to salvation/liberation are many and
varied, and it is often not easy to recognise a religious practice or a
vision of reality that is strikingly different from our own as part of
another way from ego-centredness to Reality-centredness. The
main kinds of way have long been known as the mystical way of
contemplation and knowledge, the practical way of action in the
world, and the way of loving devotion to the Real experienced as
personal. It should be noted, incidentally, that these are not to be
identified with different religions; for each of the great traditions
includes all three ways, although often in characteristically
different proportions. We should respect ways other than our
own, whether or not we truly appreciate them.

And, third, whilst we can to some extent assess and grade
religious phenomena, we cannot realistically assess and grade the
great world religions as totalities. For each of these long traditions
is so internally diverse, containing so many different kinds of both
good and evil, that it is impossible for human judgement to weigh
up and compare their merits as systems of salvation. It may be
that one facilitates human liberation/salvation more than the
others; but if so this is not evident to human vision. So far as we

can tell, they are equally productive of that transition from self to Reality which we see in the saints of all traditions.

This is a broad conclusion about the great traditions as totalities, each with a life spanning many centuries and occupying large areas of the world. However, it may well be that a great tradition constitutes in some periods of its history, and in some regions of the world, and in some of its branches or sects, a better context of salvation/liberation than in others. Thus it may well be more auspicious to be born into a given religion in one period of history than in another; and, at a given period, in one country or region rather than in another; and again, within a given period or region, into one sect or branch rather than another. And, likewise, it may well be more auspicious to be born into a good period, region, or branch of religion A than into a bad period, region, or branch of religion B. And when we come down to the concrete circumstances of each human individual, the respects in which his or her unique situation may be religiously auspicious or inauspicious are virtually unlimited and of virtually endless complexity. But amidst all this untraceable detail the broad conclusion stands that, whilst we can assess religious phenomena, we cannot assess and grade religious traditions as totalities. We can, I suggest, only acknowledge, and indeed rejoice in the fact, that the Real, the Ultimate, the Divine is known and responded to within each of these vast historical complexes, so that within each of them the gradual transformation of human existence from self-centredness to Reality-centredness is taking place.

NOTES

1. *Facing the Unfinished Task: Messages Delivered at the Congress on World Mission*, ed. J. O. Percy (Grand Rapids, Mich.: Eerdman, 1961) p. 9.
2. Ernst Troeltsch, 'The Place of Christianity among the World Religions', in *Christianity and Other Religions*, ed. J. H. Hick and B. Hebblethwaite (London: Collins; and Philadelphia: Fortress Press, 1981) p. 25.
3. Hans Küng, in *Christian Revelation and World Religions*, ed. J. Neuner (London: Burns and Oates, 1967) p. 27.
4. Probably numbering several million in the USA alone, according to Harvey Cox, *Turning East* (New York: Simon and Schuster, 1977) p. 93.
5. Quoted by Dwight M. Donaldson in *Studies in Muslim Ethics* (London: SPCK, 1963) p. 255.
6. Maha-Govinda Sutanta 59, *Digha-Nikaya*, II.250, in *Dialogues of the Buddha*, trs. T. W. and C. A. F. Rhys Davids, 4th edn (London: Luzac, 1959) p. 279.

6 On Conflicting Religious Truth-Claims*

In their article 'On Grading Religions, Seeking Truth, and Being Nice to People' (*Religious Studies*, vol. xix, pp. 75–80) Paul Griffiths and Delmas Lewis present my view of the relation between the world religions as a 'non-judgmental inclusivism' which, in the interests of harmony and goodwill, denies that the different religions make conflicting truth-claims. Indeed, according to Griffiths and Lewis, I deny that they make any truth-claims at all. Thus 'since the apparently incompatible truth-claims found in the world's major religious systems are not in fact truth-claims at all, there can be no incompatibility between them' (p. 76). And so no arguments arise and we can all be nice to each other!

It is chastening, but at the same time alarming, to realise that anyone could seriously suppose that this is what I have been trying to say, either in the article to which Griffiths and Lewis refer or in the other books and articles which I have devoted to this area of study in recent years. Let me reassure Griffiths and Lewis. The view which they attribute to me is – unintentionally of course – no more than a caricature. I must respond to it, however, lest such a caricature should do something to confuse discussion of an extremely important issue.

If we ask the straightforward question, 'Are there any disagreements of belief between people of different religions?', the answer is quite obviously 'Yes'; and in various places, including to some extent in the article 'On Grading Religions' (chapter 5 above), I have discussed some of the various levels of conflict which have to be distinguished between beliefs held by people both within different traditions and within the same tradition.

One level consists of differences of historical belief which carry

* Reprinted, with permission, from *Religious Studies*, vol. xix (1983).

significant theological implications. For example, Christians (with very few exceptions) believe that Jesus died on the cross whilst Muslims (with very few exceptions) believe that he only appeared to die. This Christian–Muslim difference has implications for those forms of atonement doctrine for which Jesus's physical death was of the essence of his atoning sacrifice. It is also to be noted that equally considerable differences of historical belief can be found within the same tradition. For example, some Christians do whilst others do not believe that Jesus had no human father. (It is, incidentally, an interesting complication of the map of differences that Muslims affirm the virgin birth of Jesus whilst many Christians today do not.) Again, some Christians do but others do not believe that Jesus's resurrection involved a revivifying of his physical corpse. On the Muslim side there is the unresolved debate about whether the prophet Muhammad did or did not appoint Ali as his successor, a difference which lies at the root of the division between Shias and Sunnis. Such historical disagreements, whether between or within traditions, could only properly be settled by historical evidence. But since they invariably refer to the events of many centuries ago, concerning which the available evidence is fragmentary and inconclusive, they usually cannot in fact be settled on purely historical grounds and tend in practice to be decided by the pull of wider theological considerations. For some believers these historical issues are fundamentally divisive, for others not. Here I would urge that we should all school ourselves to tolerate and live with such disagreements. For my part, I hold (in my arrogance) that someone who differs from me about, for example, whether Jesus had a human father is probably (though not certainly) mistaken; but in holding this I am also conscious that he/she might nevertheless be closer to the divine Reality than I. This awareness (which must always in principle be in order) is important because it has the effect of de-emphasising such differences of historical judgement. They can never be more than penultimately important.

Second, there are quasi-historical or trans-historical (though these may not be the best labels for them) differences, of which a prime example is the acceptance and rejection of the doctrine of reincarnation.[1] This is a doctrine which Hindus and Buddhists (with a few exceptions) affirm but which Christians, Jews and Muslims (with a few exceptions) reject. There are of course several different forms of reincarnation belief. But whether any of them is factually true remains extremely difficult to determine. Both empirical and conceptual issues are involved, and the consideration of these has sometimes led individuals to come to believe or to cease to believe that reincarnation occurs. I would say that we are dealing here with what is ultimately a question of fact, and that it should in theory be possible, if the weight of evidence comes to require it, either for Muslims, Jews and Christians to adopt reincarnation into their own belief-systems (as has recently been advocated by Geddes MacGregor[2]) or for Hindus and Buddhists to demythologise the belief (as has been advocated by the distinguished Thai Buddhist, Bikkhu Buddhadasa[3]). But in practice the basic question of fact is so difficult to determine that it may well go on being discussed and disagreed about for a very long time or even for the rest of earthly history. In the meantime it is, I would suggest, an issue on which we should learn to tolerate differences. One should be able to recognise that a person who accepts reincarnation when one denies it, or who denies it when one affirms it, might nevertheless be closer to the divine Reality than one is oneself; and therefore that if someone is mistaken on this matter the mistake cannot be of ultimate importance. This is not to deny its genuine significance and its extensive ramifying implications; but nevertheless to know now whether we do or do not live again on earth is evidently not essential to our salvation or liberation.

However it would I think be possible, over a sufficient period of time, for Buddhism (or for part of the Buddhist world) to come to see reincarnation as a mythological rather than a literal truth; or for Christianity (or part of the Christian world) to come to accept reincarnation as an historical fact, affecting either all or some people. Such developments would of course have wide reverberations throughout their respective belief-systems. Their total pictures of the world would undergo a shift. But change is of the essence of life; and equally large shifts have already taken place within both Buddhist and Christian history – in Buddhism in the development of the Mahāyāna, and in Christianity in the assimilation of the modern scientific outlook and of the scientific study of the scriptures.

Third, on a higher and more momentous level, there are differences in the ways of conceiving and experiencing, and hence also of responding to, the divine Reality. The major division is of course that between the awareness of the divine as personal and awareness of it as non-personal. It is at this point that we have to opt for some general theory of the relation between these claimed awarenesses of the divine. There are, I think, three main possibilities, which can be aptly labelled the 'exclusivist', the 'inclusivist', and the 'pluralist' understandings of the religious situation. By 'exclusivism' I mean the view that one particular mode of religious thought and experience (namely, one's own) is alone valid, all others being false. By 'inclusivism' I mean the view (advocated by Karl Rahner in his influential theory of 'anonymous Christianity' and largely adopted, though without use of that term, by Vatican II) that one's own tradition alone has the whole truth but that this truth is nevertheless partially reflected in other traditions; and, as an additional clause special to Christianity, that whilst salvation is made possible only by the death of Christ, the benefits of this are available to all mankind (a position adopted by the present Pope in his Encyclical *Redemptor Hominis*, 1979, para. 14). And by 'pluralism' I mean the view – which I advocate – that the great world faiths embody different perceptions and conceptions of, and correspondingly different responses to, the Real or the Ultimate from within the different cultural ways of being human; and that within each of them the transformation of human existence from self-centredness to Reality-centredness is manifestly taking place.

Griffiths and Lewis present the practical need for the mutual acceptance of human beings in an emerging world community as the decisive issue in the minds of those who reject religious exclusivism. There is certainly an enormously important issue here. But there is also a profoundly important religious dimension. When I meet a devout Jew, or Muslim, or Sikh, or Hindu, or Buddhist in whom the fruits of openness to the divine Reality are gloriously evident, I cannot realistically regard the Christian experience of the divine as authentic and their non-Christian experiences as inauthentic. It is of course possible to maintain that religion is, *in toto*, illusion and projection. However I do not believe this. And it would be grotesquely arbitrary and parochial to confine one's rejection of the naturalistic interpretation of religious experience to that occurring within one's own tradition. The philosophical Golden Rule requires us to extend the same principle to others that we apply to ourselves.

We start then, from a religious point of view, with a range of

forms of religious experience and thought which we do not reject
as illusory but which on the contrary we have accepted as
constituting different human (and therefore necessarily limited
and imperfect) perceptions of the divine. And we need a theory
which enables us to be uninhibitedly fascinated by the immense
range of differences between these perceptions whilst at the same
time seeing them as constituting our varied human responses to a
transcendent divine Reality. The theory which I have elsewhere
tentatively suggested hinges on the distinction between the Real
an sich (in him/her/itself) and the Real as humanly thought and
experienced. (In different forms this distinction is familiar within
each of the great traditions: as *nirguṇa* and *saguṇa* Brahman; as *en
Soph* or *al Haqq* in distinction from the self-revealing God of the
Torah or the Qur'ān; as the *dharmakāya*, on the one hand, and the
sambhogakāya and *nirmāṇakāya* on the other; as the Godhead (*deitas*)
and God (*deus*); as God in his eternal self-existent being and God
as related to and known by his creatures.) To this distinction we
have to add the basic epistemological principle, introduced into
modern European thought by Kant but confirmed and developed
in modern psychology, sociology of knowledge and the philosophy
of science, that we are always aware of reality beyond ourselves in
terms of the sets of concepts which structure our own cognitive
consciousness. And the different religious traditions, with their
different conceptual systems, methods of worship or meditation,
and life-styles, nourished as they are by different scriptures and
supported by their respective communal matrices, constitute the
'lenses' through which different human faith-communities variously perceive the divine Reality. The two basic concepts which
are central to the different forms of religious experience are the
concept of deity, or of the Real as personal, and the concept of the
absolute, or of the Real as non-personal. These take particular
concrete forms at different human interfaces with the divine, as
the divine *personae* (Yahweh, Shiva, Vishnu, the heavenly Father,
the Qur'ānic Revealer, and so on) and the divine *impersonae* (such
as Brahman, the Tao, *nirvāṇa*, *śūnyatā*, the *dharmakāya*).

This is – obviously – not to say that the different conceptions or
images of the Real are phenomenologically the same. Nor is it to
say that the different expectations concerning the ultimate state,
expressed in such concepts as heaven and *nirvāṇa*, are the same.
What is the same, though taking many different forms, is the
transformation of human existence from self-centredness to

Reality-centredness. It is this, in my view, that lies at the heart of the different conceptions of salvation and liberation, both Western and Eastern.

Given some such general theory as this, the differences and disagreements between the religious traditions can be seen as entirely real and yet as not requiring religious exclusivism, or even inclusivism. For the authenticity of, for example, the Christian awareness of the Real as our Heavenly Father, by living within which awareness human beings are transformed from self-centredness to Reality-centredness, does not exclude or conflict with the authenticity of the Muslim awareness of the Real as Allah the Merciful, the Compassionate, or with the vaishnavite Hindu awareness of the Real as the loving Lord of the *Bhagavad Gita*. The fact that one religious way leads to salvation/liberation does not entail that another way fails to do so.

Griffiths and Lewis cite, as a good example of conflicting truth-claims, the Christian belief that God exists and has created the world, in contrast with the Buddhist belief that 'the universe is created by karmic effect' (p. 78). (A Buddhist might well have reservations about this latter formulation.) The general example is one around which much discussion has centred, and reveals a difference which is more complex, and perhaps more interesting, than Griffiths and Lewis's reference to it might suggest. One of the most learned Western students of Buddhism, Edward Conze, concluded that 'the Buddhists adopt an attitude of agnosticism to the question of a personal creator'.[4] For the Buddha treated the question of whether the universe had a beginning (in which case it may have been created by some power other than itself) or is eternal, as a question to which we do not need to know the answer; and he discouraged his disciples from bothering about such matters. Why? 'It is because it is not connected with the goal, is not fundamental to Brahma-faring, and does not conduce to the turning away from, nor to dispassion, stopping, calming, super-knowledge, awakening nor nibbāna.'[5]

Indeed it seems to me that the Buddha's doctrine of the undetermined questions, to know the answers to which is not necessary for liberation, is one which non-Buddhists also could adopt with profit. And it may well be among such questions that the conflicting truth-claims of the different traditions occur. Such differences are often indeed of great philosophical importance as elements within our respective theories about the universe; but they are not of great *religious*, i.e. soteriological, importance. For different groups can hold incompatible sets of theories all of which constitute intellectual frameworks within which the process of salvation/liberation can proceed.

Thus a Christian and a Buddhist, if they come to accept a pluralistic point of view, will be able to differ peacefully in their theories and in the modes of experience which these theories make possible. The Buddhist will be able to acknowledge that the ultimate Reality, which he or she has conceived and experienced in the light of the Buddha's teaching, is very differently conceived and experienced by Christians. And the Christian will be able to acknowledge that the Real, which he or she has encountered as the divine Thou, is known by Buddhists as the ineffable 'further shore' of *nirvāṇa*; or the eternal Buddha-nature (*dharmakāya*); or the ultimate Emptiness (*śūnyatā*) which is also the fullness or suchness of the world, the ultimate reality of everything, that which gives final meaning and joy. And both will affirm the ultimate Reality, beyond human picturing, which is the ground of both forms of experience.

If we now ask ourselves how it can be that the same ultimate divine Reality can be perceived in such different ways from within the different religions, yet all producing the same basic human transformation, the answer must involve both the infinity of the divine Reality, transcending all our conceptualisations, and the historical variety of the human cultures which form the lenses through which that Reality is variously perceived.

It is only now, against the background of a general theory of the relation between the religious traditions, that the question of grading arises. For clearly it is in principle possible that some of the religious 'lenses' through which the Real is perceived may be more adequate than others. And indeed each tradition has in fact normally believed that this is so, and that it itself constitutes the most adequate, or the only fully adequate, window onto the divine. In the article 'On Grading Religions' I made a number of suggestions for criteria by which to assess particular religious phenomena – the founding figures, systems of doctrine, mythologies, social and historical out-workings – and I shall not repeat these here. I concluded that 'whilst we can to some extent assess and grade religious phenomena, we cannot realistically assess and grade the great world religions as totalities. For each of these long traditions is so internally diverse, containing so many kinds of both good and evil, that it is impossible for human judgement to weigh them up and compare their merits as systems of salvation. It may be that one facilitates human liberation/salvation more than the others; but if so this is not evident to human vision'.

To revert now to the questions raised by Griffiths and Lewis, I would say that the differences of belief between (and within) the traditions are legion, but that it is important to distinguish their various levels. These include differences of historical fact, which are in principle settleable now though in practice often not; differences of what might be called metaphysical fact (e.g. reincarnation), which are settleable eschatologically but probably not now; and differences of mythology and doctrinal interpretation, constituting systems which may well be analogous to alternative maps, in different projections, of the universe. These different differences both arise from and help to constitute different perceptions of the divine from within different forms of human life. They concern questions to which we cannot realistically claim at present to know the answers and about which a variety of speculations, images and stories are possible. Such theories and mythologies are not however necessary for salvation/liberation, the transformation of human existence from self-centredness to Reality-centredness. They are of course endlessly fascinating to many of us; indeed we make our living out of them! But we might perhaps nevertheless do well to ponder the Buddha's teaching that they do not conduce to liberation. They are less than ultimately important.

NOTES

1. For more about this, see my article in *Truth and Dialogue*, ed. John Hick (London: Sheldon Press; and Philadelphia: Westminster Press, 1974); and my *Death and Eternal Life* (London: Collins; New York: Harper and Row, 1976. Revised, London: Macmillan, 1985) chs 16–19.

2. Geddes MacGregor, *Reincarnation as a Christian Hope* (London: Macmillan; New York: Barnes and Noble, 1982).

3. Bikkhu Buddhadasa, in *Towards the Truth*, ed. Donald Swearer (Philadelphia: Westminster Press, 1972).

4. Edward Conze, *Buddhism: Its Essence and Development*, 3rd edn (Oxford: Cassirer, 1957) p. 39.

5. S. *Majjhima-Nikāya*, 1.431, in *The Middle-Length Sayings*, vol. II, trs. I. B. Horner (London: Lzuac, 1957) p. 101.

7 In Defence of Religious Pluralism

I*

I am grateful to Dr Philip Almond ('John Hick's Copernican Theology', *Theology*, January 1983) for undertaking something of a cost–benefit analysis of the pluralistic approach to the theology of religions. He sees very clearly both the way in which a pluralistic theory would, as its main benefit, illuminate the otherwise baffling relationship between the great world traditions, and also the way in which it would, as its inevitable cost, involve a radical reinterpretation of some central Christian concepts.

Almond refers to the ancient parable of the blind men and the elephant. Each of them touches a different part of the animal, the one who feels a leg mistakenly identifying the elephant as a tree, the one who feels the trunk identifying it as a snake, and so on. Likewise – the parable suggests – the different religious traditions have mistakenly developed dogmatic definitions of the divine on the assumption that their own partial experience of it is complete and adequate. The parable is useful so long as one does not read into it more than is intended. For example, the blind men grasp different *parts* of the elephant. But when a Muslim speaks of Allah the Qur'ānic revealer, and a Hindu speaks of Brahman as the limitless transpersonal consciousness, they are not referring to two *parts* of reality but to two ways in which the limitless divine reality has been thought and experienced by different human mentalities forming and formed by different intellectual frameworks and devotional techniques. This particular limitation of the parable is appreciated by Almond. However, he now

* 'The Theology of Pluralism', *Theology*, vol. LXXXVI, no. 713 (September 1983), reprinted with permission.

comments: 'The central assumption of the parable is that Hick is in a position to see whereas the blind religions are not' (p. 37). But this is to mistake the nature of a hypothesis. I cannot speak for the ancient seers who first told this parable; but those of us who sometimes cite it today use it simply as a vivid expository device to express an hypothesis about the relationship between the great religious traditions. We do not, needless to say, pretend to a cosmic vantage-point from which one could observe both the divine Reality in itself and the different partial human awarenesses of that Reality. The hypothesis of an ultimate divine noumenon which is humanly experienced as a range of divine phenomena is arrived at inductively. We start from the phenomenological data of the forms of religious experience and thought presented by the history of religion. We then seek to interpret these data from the standpoint of the basic conviction that religious experience is not, as such and *in toto*, a realm of illusory projection but is also, at least in part, an effect within human consciousness of the presence and pressure of a transcendent divine Reality. Thus the aim of the hypothesis is to formulate a religious, as distinguished from a naturalistic, understanding of religion. For it is the basic assumption of every believer that he or she is in touch, even if imperfectly and 'as through a glass, darkly', with a higher reality. And when we extend this assumption to other religious traditions than our own we have before us the range of data interpreted by the elephant-and-blind-men hypothesis. This does not profess to be the report of a cosmic vision, but to be the theory which best makes sense of the facts of religion from a religious rather than a naturalistic point of view. Rather than speaking of claims to a privileged vantage-point an appropriate critical response would be to offer a better hypothesis.

We now come to some terminological troubles. Using characteristically theistic language, I have spoken of the ultimate divine reality as everywhere 'revealing' itself to human beings, this universal revelatory activity being differently perceived and responded to within the different cultural ways of being human. Almond rightly points out that the term 'revelation' is much more at home within the theistic that the non-theistic traditions. I have tried to use it, however, in a wider sense which does not necessarily entail divinely disclosed propositions or miraculous interventions in the course of human history, but in which all authentic religious awareness is a response to the circumambient presence and prevenient pressure of the divine Reality. I can see the point, however, of the suggestion that the language of revelation is out of place in discussions of religious pluralism. But a more serious terminological problem centres on the word 'God'. I have tried to use it in such a way that it is proper to ask whether God is personal. But I accept that this usage can easily be misunderstood. I therefore prefer to speak of 'the Real', and to distinguish between human experience of the Real as personal (taking such concrete forms as Yahweh, Shiva, Vishnu, the Heavenly Father) and of the Real as non-personal (taking such forms as Brahman, the Tao, the Dharma, *nirvāṇa*, *śūnyatā*).

I do not think that it is correct, but on the contrary misleading, to identify such a view as 'fundamentally a Vedāntin solution' (p. 39). It differs importantly from advaita Vedānta, in which, as Almond says, 'all differences are, so to say, swallowed up within the impersonal absolute being Brahman' (p. 38). For (as he acknowledges) the view that the Real is equally authentically thought and experienced as personal and as non-personal is importantly different from this advaitist position. And it is equally different from the visistādvaitist view that Brahman is ultimately personal. It is, I would suggest, essential to learn a basic lesson that Kant has taught us, namely that *all* human awareness of reality transcending ourselves involves the use of interpretative concepts. This truth has to be applied not only to sense-experience but also (going beyond Kant) to religious experience. And the evidence of religious experience throughout the world is that the Real can be experienced both in terms of the concept of deity and in terms of the concept of the absolute, each concept being (to use Kantian language) 'schematised' within actual human experience as a variety of historical *personae* and ahistorical *impersonae*. There is, I think, an illuminating analogy here with the use of the complementarity principle in relation to electromagnetic radiations.[1] When light is experimented upon in a certain way it exhibits wave-like properties, and when experimented upon it another way, particle-like properties. We have to say that in itself, independently of interaction with human observers, it is such as to be capable of being experienced under different experimental conditions in these different ways. Analogously, a religious tradition is a way of 'experimenting' in relation to the divine. Its system of concepts, its method of prayer or meditation, its supporting scriptures, the whole formative influence of its community and tradition, constitute a complex 'lens' through which the divine reality is perceived in a certain light and as having a certain shape. Through dualistic–personalist lenses the real is seen and responded to as personal; through monistic lenses, as non-personal. And so we postulate the Real *an sich*, concerning which we have to say that it is capable of being authentically thought and experienced by human beings in these two significantly different ways; and within each way under a variety of different concrete experienceable forms.

At the end of his article Almond raises a further issue. It is only in the eschaton that the varying and often conflicting truth-claims of the different traditions could be finally adjudicated in the light of a definitive and universal experience of the divine Reality. It *may* then become clear that a 'Ptolemaic' Christian (or Muslim, or Hindu, or other) faith is true after all, according to which that particular faith alone has taught the truth and constituted the only effective way of salvation. Perhaps it will be eschatologically verified, for example, that 'there is no other name given under heaven whereby men may be saved' than the name of Jesus, and that only those who have accepted him as their lord and saviour can escape eternal condemnation. So long as this is *possible*, can we ask those who believe such exclusive dogmas to move from a Jesus-centred to a God-centred, or Reality-centred, picture? 'Is it reasonable to demand a Copernican revolution of this sort while the possibility remains that, in the final eschatological analysis, it may turn out that a Ptolemaic Christian theology of some sort or other was theologically valid?' (Almond, pp. 39–40)

Now on the one hand it must be granted that it is logically possible (i.e. not a self-contradictory idea) that some one particular 'Ptolemaic' religious vision does correspond uniquely with how things are. But on the other hand the whole problem of religious pluralism has arisen, for Western thinkers, from recognising the prohibitive cost of the old Christian presumption of a monopoly of the saving truth. This presumption generated the paradox of a God of universal love who has ordained that only the Christian minority of the human race can be saved. It is precisely this paradox that has called for a 'Copernican revolution' in our Christian theology of religions. And it would be unreasonable to refuse such a reconceptualisation simply on the ground that it is *logically possible* that it is mistaken. It is logically possible that *any* conceptuality, in any field, is mistaken; but if this prevented us from acting on any hypothesis, however well grounded, we should be paralysed – in ordinary daily life, in science, and in religion. I therefore suggest that the mere fact that it is always logically possible that our understanding may be mistaken should not prevent us from proceeding upon the best understanding that we have. Putting it the other way round, the mere fact that it may conceivably be true that, for example, 'no one remaining outside the Catholic Church, not just pagans, but also Jews or heretics or schismatics, can become partakers of eternal life; but they will go to the "everlasting fire which was prepared for the devil and his angels", unless before the end of life they are joined to the Church',[2] should not outweigh the many positive reasons that we have for thinking that this is not in fact true.

A more probable 'eschatological scenario' (for which I have offered some supporting considerations in *Death and Eternal Life*) might be one in which we move in stages towards the ultimate relationship to or union with the divine, and that as we approach nearer to that consummation our conceptions of 'how things are' will gradually become more adequate. It seems likely that in this process many of the ideas embedded within each of the religious traditions will become variously modified or marginalised or superseded. It does, of course, remain logically possible that some present set of dogmas (Catholic or Protestant, Mormon or Seventh Day Adventist, Sunni or Shia, Theravāda or Mahāyāna, advaitist or visistādvaitist) will turn out to correspond precisely with reality; but in view of the manifest human cultural contributions to all of these sets of ideas it seems *more* likely that all of them will, in varying degrees, have to undergo correction or enlargement or transformation of the light of fuller experience.

It therefore seems to me that the bare logical possibility that the picture of reality taught by some group or individual *may* turn out to be 'the truth, the whole truth, and nothing but the truth' should not deter us from adopting, as considerably more probable, the pluralistic hypothesis that the great world faiths represent different conceptions and perceptions of, and correspondingly different responses to, the one ultimate divine Reality.

If we do adopt this kind of hypothesis, then it is certainly true that, as Almond says, it will have implications for the development of Christian theology, and hence for Christian liturgies, and also for practical Christian attitudes towards non-Christian human beings. However, we are all conscious today that the

Christian tradition is a living organism which has grown and changed through the centuries in response to changes in its environment and that it must go on growing and changing in the future. Today Western Christianity finds itself in a new historical environment in which it is inevitably becoming conscious of itself, no longer as the one-and-only but now as one-among-several. (In some other parts of the world this consciousness has long existed, although the Christian response to it has too often been dictated from the West.) The developments of Christian outlook, belief, and practice which are called for in a consciously pluralistic world can only become clear through prolonged thought and discussion, debate and argument, reflection and heart-searching on the part of the present and, perhaps even more, the next generation of Christian thinkers. This is an aspect of the continual process of death and resurrection by which alone a religion remains vital. Thus if, for example, the idea of divine incarnation comes to be seen as having metaphorical rather than literal truth, and if the policy of converting the world to Christianity comes to be seen as an anachronistic by-product of a past imperial age, the changes involved will be as great as, but probably no greater than, those brought about a hundred years ago by the impact of modern biology and the historical study of the scriptures.

Christianity is of course not the only religion that has to discover how to move from a one-and-only to a one-among-several self-understanding. For each of the great traditions has developed its own absolute claim which in principle relegates other revelations and ways of salvation to a secondary status. To varying extents the kind of rethinking that is going on fairly vigorously within Christianity is also going on within the other major traditions; and the gradually emerging outcome will be a new pluralistic world consciousness. But the rethinking has to be done *within* each tradition, developing its own resources in the direction of the pluralistic vision. It is not for Christians to try to tell Muslims, for example, how they should develop their own theology; or *vice versa*. We can, however, all help and encourage one another by engaging in the world-wide network of inter-faith dialogue. The new experiences which this brings can often create a powerful impetus to the painful/exciting/bewildering/illuminating work of reconceptualisation and the creation of new relationships.

II*

I am grateful to Mr Peter Byrne ('John Hick's Philosophy of World Religions', *Scottish Journal of Theology*, vol. xxxv, pp. 289–301) for highlighting some of the central issues for a philosophy of religious pluralism. He starts from the now widespread realisation that it is not a morally or religiously acceptable view that salvation depends upon being a member of the Christian minority within the human race. A more realistic view must be pluralistic, seeing the great religious traditions as different ways of conceiving and experiencing the one ultimate divine Reality, and correspondingly different ways of responding to that Reality. These ways owe their differences to the modes of thinking, perceiving and feeling which have developed within the different patterns of human existence embodied in the various cultures of the earth. Thus, on the one hand the religions are responses to a single ultimate transcendent Reality, whilst on the other hand their several communal consciousnesses of that Reality, formed from different human perspectives, are widely different. To understand this mixture of commonality and difference I have suggested that we should make use of a basic distinction which occurs in some form within each of the great traditions. In Christian terms it is the distinction between God-in-himself, in his eternal self-existing being, independently of creation, and God-for-us or God as revealed to us. In more universal language it is the distinction between the Real (*Sat, al Haqq*) *an sich* and the Real as humanly experienced and thought. And it is the latter – the Real-for-us – that is known under different forms within different streams of human life. This basic distinction opens up the possibility of a religious, as opposed to a naturalistic or atheistic, understanding of the facts of religious plurality.

The perennial controversy between a religious and a naturalistic interpretation of religion is central to Mr Byrne's article. He asks, very properly, why we should hold that the great traditions are all in different ways true rather than being all in different ways false? The answer has to come in two stages. The first is a defence of the basic religious conviction that religious thought and experience is not, as such, a matter of delusion and projection but

* 'The Philosophy of World Religions', *Scottish Journal of Theology*, vol. xxxvii, no. 2 (1984), reprinted with permission.

mediates a real contact with a higher Reality beyond us. This is not to say that there are no distorting human factors within our religious awareness. Any candid student of the history of religions will recognise in it a considerable human element affecting the particular forms that religious consciousness has taken. But the basic religious conviction is that in and through these humanly conditioned modes of awareness and response there has been a genuine impact of transcendent divine Reality upon human life. This conviction is basic, regardless of whether it is held that there is one and only one valid form of religion, or several.

It is accordingly not the purpose of a philosophy of religious pluralism to provide the 'safeguard against atheism' (p. 299) which Mr Byrne wants. The controversy with atheism centres upon the rationality or otherwise of the basic religious conviction. If an erstwhile atheist should become convinced that there is a transcendent divine Reality, it does not seem likely that he or she will then be unable to come to terms with the evident fact that this Reality is varyingly conceived and experienced by different kinds of human mentality.

Nevertheless Mr Byrne is right in insisting that this plurality does have to be given a reasonable interpretation. And so the second stage of the answer, once it is granted that it can be rational to live and to believe on the basis of a stream of religious experience and thought, deals with the plurality of these streams. For, if it is rational for the Christian to believe in God on the basis of his or her distinctively Christian experience, it must by the same argument be rational for the Muslim to believe in the reality of Allah on the basis of distinctively Islamic experience, and for the Hindu and the Buddhist to believe in the reality of Brahman, the Dharma, the eternal Buddha, *nirvāṇa*, *śūnyatā*, on the basis of their own distinctive forms of experience. But how can this be? If one community is authentically experiencing the divine Reality as the Yahweh of Israel, can another community be authentically experiencing that Reality as the Allah of the Qur'ānic revelation, whilst yet another community is experiencing this same divine Reality as the non-personal Brahman, and yet another as the eternal Dharma or as the ineffable Void which is also the Suchness and the inner meaning of the world? This is the central problem addressed by a philosophy of religious pluralism.

The broad answer which I have suggested is arrived at inductively. We start from the phenomenological fact of the various forms of religious experience, and we seek an hypothesis which will make sense of this realm of phenomena from the point of view of the basic religious conviction that religious experience is not pure projection or hallucination but is, or at least includes, a real encounter with transcendent divine Reality. The theory that most naturally suggests itself postulates a divine Reality which is in itself limitless, exceeding the scope of human conceptuality and language, but which is humanly thought and experienced in various conditioned and limited ways. It is thought and experienced both under the general concept of Deity, or the Real as personal, historically concretised within different streams of religious experience as Yahweh, Vishnu, Shiva, Allah, the Heavenly Father, and so on; and also under the general concept of the absolute, or the Real as non-personal, concretised as Brahman, the Dharma, the Tao, the *dharmakāya*, *nirvāṇa*, *śūnyatā*, and so forth. Around these different ways of conceiving, experiencing and responding to the Real there have grown up the various religious traditions of the world with their myths and symbols, their philosophies and theologies, their liturgies and arts, their ethics and life-styles. Within all of them basically the same salvific process is taking place, namely the transformation of human existence from self-centredness to Reality-centredness. Each of the great traditions thus constitutes a valid context of salvation/ liberation; but none constitutes the one and only such context, and each may be able to gain a larger understanding of the Real by attending to the reports and conceptualities of the others.

Given such a theory it would be misleading to describe the distinction between the Real *an sich* and the Real as humanly experienced (as Mr Byrne does) as a distinction between reality and mere appearance. For all our awareness of reality, of every kind, is necessarily an awareness of it as it appears to – i.e. is experienced by – us. We see this very clearly at the physical level where perception involves sense-organs and a nervous-system. Our own human perceptual machinery differs from a horse's or a bird's or an ant's. Accordingly the world as humanly perceived must be different from the world as perceived by ants, birds and horses. And neither we nor they perceive the swirling cloud of sub-atomic particles or the basic quanta of discharging energy described by the physicists, presumably because to do so would not be biologically useful to us. We necessarily perceive the world as it appears to beings with our own particular kind of perceptual machinery. But the way in which it appears to human perceivers is the way it *is* in relation to human perceivers. In Kantian language, the phenomenal world *is* the noumenal world, as humanly experienced.

When we turn from our physical to our social environment, and again to our supposed more ultimate divine environment, we have to take account not only of the sense-organs and brain but also of the structures of concepts in terms of which we unconsciously interpret and then consciously experience. It is at this level that a pluralistic theory becomes inevitable. For we have become irreversibly aware in the present century, as a result of anthropological, sociological and psychological studies and of work in the philosophy of language, that there is no one universal and invariable set of human interpretative concepts, but rather a range of significantly different such sets which have developed throughout the wide diversity of the forms of human life.

It is not, then (as Mr Byrne suggests), the presumed infinity of the divine Reality that leads to differing conceptions of it. It would be conceivable (though unlikely) for everyone to have a similar limited understanding of an unlimited being. The infinity of the Real, which is presumed both in Christianity and in all the other major religious traditions, is inferred rather than experienced and is closely connected with the idea of ultimacy. I think that the inference to unlimitedness is a good one. But in relation to religious pluralism the issue is not divine infinity versus divine finitude. It is enough to hold, on inductive grounds, that the Reality to which the major forms of religious experience point has a richer nature than is witnessed to by any one tradition alone. For example, that Reality is such as to be authentically experienced both as personal and as transpersonal: it is the postulated ground both of the experienced Yahweh and of the experienced Brahman. The variety of conceptions and perceptions of (and hence of responses to) the divine Reality flows from the two circumstances: (1) that the conceptual schema and constructive operations of the mind enter into all human consciousness of reality, divine as well as natural; and (2) that there is not just one way of being human, with just one pattern of interpretative concepts, but a number of ways which have developed within the major cultural streams and which have produced human beings with capacities and liabilities to become conscious of the Real in distinctively different ways.

Given this kind of theory, the sceptical question posed by Mr

Byrne now arises. If the ultimate divine Reality can be humanly known only in various imperfect and culturally conditioned ways, on what grounds can we claim that behind these varied religious phenomena lies an unexperienceable divine noumenon? The answer is that we *postulate* that noumenon in affirming the basic conviction that religious experience is not, as such, an illusory projection of our imaginations. The conviction that religious experience is not caused solely by human factors, but also by the impact upon us of a transcendent Reality, leads to the theory of an ultimate divine noumenon which is humanly known as a range of divine phenomena.

If this is accepted, attention moves to the question of criteria for judging the adequacy of different human perceptions of the Real. For it is of course theoretically possible that one particular human tradition constitutes a lens through which the Real is perceived fully and without distortion, and accordingly rightly responded to, whilst through the others the Real is in various ways and degrees distorted and therefore wrongly responded to. This is indeed not only the traditional Christian claim, but equally the traditional Muslim, Jewish, Hindu and Buddhist claim – each of course seeing itself as the one and only true lens! But the connection between perception and response leads to a critique of this assumption. For if we grant that the central concern of religion is salvation or liberation – the transformation of human existence from self-centredness to Reality-centredness – then we shall have to acknowledge that this transformation seems to be taking place within the contexts of each of the great traditions. Can we perhaps, however, show that it is taking place more extensively, or more intensively, within one particular tradition; or that its social outworking within one tradition is superior to its social outworking within the others? Such questions require detailed discussion; but the correct conclusion, I believe, is that, whilst we can to some extent assess particular religious phenomena by rational and ethical criteria, the great religious traditions as totalities have each taken so many different forms, and have such complex histories, with their own different periods of flourishing and of recession and their distinctive strengths and weaknesses, that global assessments are impossible. Each is an unique historical mixture of good and evil, and human judgement lacks the wisdom and impartiality to grade them. When we see a stream of religious life which has existed for many centuries, which has produced profound scriptures, saints in whom the transition to Reality-centredness is far advanced, and impressive intellectual systems, and has provided a successful framework of life for hundreds of millions of people and the basis of at least one major human civilisation, I believe that we must presume that it is built upon an authentic human perception of the Real.

A philosophy of religious pluralism such as I have outlined has some not unimportant advantages, both academic and religious.

Academically, to acknowledge the unavoidable cultural element within the forms of religion frees us to observe and to be fascinated by the differences between the different traditions, without any pressure to homogenise them or to depict the objects of religious experience – Yahweh, Brahman, Shiva, the Holy Trinity, *śūnyatā*, the Dharma, and so on – as phenomenologically alike. Thus within this theory the historical and phenomenological study of religion can flourish freely. We are also enabled to acknowledge realistically the element of human projection within religious consciousness and, as a corollary, the possibility of perverted forms of religious experience and practice, both within and outside the great traditions. There is no pressure to suppose that religion is always or necessarily good!

A further consequence is an understanding of religious dogmas and doctrines as not, for the most part, straightforward assertions of fact but as complex mixtures of the mythical, the symbolic, the philosophical and the empirical. They are therefore not to be judged as though they were very large-scale scientific statements, but by the extent to which, as conceptual systems, they provide a framework within which the transformation of human existence from self-centredness to Reality-centredness can take place. In this connection I think that Mr Byrne exaggerates the importance of doctrinal agreement when he says that 'whether two men worship the same thing or not depends not so much on similarity in how they respond *to* that thing, but rather in there being a sufficient similarity in what they say *about* that thing' (pp. 293–4). But different descriptions, formed within different observational contexts, may refer to the same reality: as in the famous case of the Morning Star and the Evening Star, which were once assumed to be different stars but are now known to be the same. Again, it has been quite possible for different people to respond to a great religious figure – say, Mahatma Gandhi – in terms of very different conceptualities, one seeing him as a political leader

making a total moral demand for the sake of Indian independence; another seeing him as a saint of non-violent love,
challenging others to attain the same level of *ahimsa*; and another
seeing him, in Hindu theological terms, as a divine avatar. There
have been people whose lives were changed in essentially the same
way through responses to Gandhi made possible by these different
conceptualisations of him. It is of course true that yet others saw
him in ways – for example, as a wily politician in no way to be
admired or emulated – which did not lead to any spiritual
transformation. But among the ways of seeing him which did
change people it is not necessarily the case that one conceptuality
was true and the others false. It could be that the Hindu
mythology of the avatars, and the moral principle of *ahimsa*, and
the political demand for the dignity of independence, all offered
ways in which people could respond to a very significant but very
complex human reality. And on the much larger and more
ultimate scale it may be that different conceptualisations of the
Real – Christian, Buddhist, Muslim, Hindu, and so on – may
enable people to begin the transformation from self-centredness to
Reality-centredness. It may be that, in the words of the Muslim
mystic Rumi, 'the lamps are different but the Light is the same'.
For the basic religious conviction is not that a particular human
conceptuality corresponds literally to the limitless divine Reality,
but that through a particular such historical system (such as that
of Christianity) the human self is effectively opened to the Real
and transforming religious experience and life made possible.

Religiously, freedom from the assumption that there is one and
only one true religion makes possible a genuine appreciation of
other responses to the Real. Encounter with persons of another
tradition is now no longer coloured by the *a priori* conviction that
their faith must be inferior to one's own. Authentic dialogue of the
'truth-seeking' kind, in which each participant may gain from the
experience and insights of the others, becomes feasible. In the
light of such a philosophy the relationship between the great
traditions can be placed upon a realistic basis instead of consisting
in interactions between groups each of which regards itself as
religiously superior to the others. To a great extent the actual
attitudes of Christians in inter-faith dialogue, since both Vatican
II and the work of the World Council of Churches' Programme on
Dialogue with People of Living Faiths and Ideologies, have been
implicitly pluralistic, treating the other world religions in practice

as valid alternative contexts of salvation. But this attitude, evident at the personal level and in official inter-faith dialogue, has not yet worked back either into the structure of Christian theology or into an accepted philosophy of religious pluralism. We do, however, need such a philosophy; and those who are dissatisfied with the suggestions being made by the rather few who are actively at work in this field should consider what alternative proposals they can offer.

NOTES

1. Cf. Ian Barbour, *Myths, Models and Paradigms* (New York: Harper and Row, and London: SCM, 1974) ch. 5.
2. Decree of the Council of Florence, 1438–45, Denzinger, no. 714. Quoted from *The Church Teaches: Documents of the Church in English* (New York: Herder and Herder, 1955) p. 165.

8 Eschatological Verification Reconsidered*

I

The world in which we find ourselves is religiously ambiguous. It is possible for different people (as also for the same person at different times) to experience it both religiously and non-religiously; and to hold beliefs which arise from and feed into each of these ways of experiencing. A religious person may report that in moments of prayer he or she is conscious of existing in the unseen presence of God, and is aware – sometimes at least – that his/her whole life and the entire history of the world is taking place within the ambience of the divine purpose. But on the other hand the majority of people in our modern world do not participate in that form of experience and are instead conscious of their own and others' lives as purely natural phenomena, so that their own experience leads them at least implicitly to reject the idea of a transcendent divine presence and purpose. If they are philosophically minded, they may well think that the believer's talk is the expression of what Richard Hare has called a *blik*, a way of feeling and thinking about the world which expresses itself in pseudo-assertions, pseudo because they are neither verifiable nor falsifiable and are therefore factually empty.[1] The religious person speaks of God as a living reality in whose presence we are, and of a divine purpose which gives ultimate meaning to our lives. But is not the world the same whether or not we suppose it to exist in God's presence; and is not the course of history the same whether or not we describe it as fulfilling God's purposes? Is not the religious description thus merely a gratuitous embellishment, a logical fifth wheel, an optional language-game which may assuage some psychological need of the speaker but which involves no claims of substance concerning the objective nature or structure of the universe? Must not the central religious use of language then

* Reprinted, with permission, from *Religious Studies*, vol. XIII (1977).

be accounted a non-cognitive use, whose function is not to assert alleged facts but to express a speaker's, or a community of speakers', emotions within the framework of a factually contentless *blik*, 'slant' or 'onlook'?

The logical positivists of the 1920s and 1930s expressed this by saying that since such sentences as 'God loves mankind' are neither analytically true nor empirically verifiable they must be cognitively meaningless. They asked how God-talk could be verified; and most of the responses which they received from the theological world amounted to a repudiation of the question rather than an answer to it. Later, Antony Flew in the 'Theology and Falsification' debate asked whether such sentences as 'God loves mankind' are falsifiable – that is, such that if they are false they could ever be discovered to be so.[2] What conceivable state of affairs, he asked, would show that there is no loving God? He was given two kinds of answer. One was the non-cognitivist response, embodied in Hare's concept of the *blik* and in R. B. Braithwaite's account of religious belief as a disguised expression of intention to live according to a certain ethical pattern.[3] Such answers share the assumption that religious beliefs are cognitively empty. The other response was the cognitivist answer formulated in different ways by Basil Mitchell[4] and Ian Crombie.[5] These both point implicitly or explicitly, as it seems to me, to some notion of eschatological verification for their further development; and it is this notion that I want to discuss here.

The broad idea is that the theistic conception of the universe, and of what is going on in human life, *is* capable of experiential verification, although according to Christianity the verifying situation lies in the final fulfilment of God's purpose for us beyond this present life. Perhaps I may be allowed to repeat here a parable in which I have previously embodied this general idea, before going on to its more precise elaboration.

Two people are travelling together along a road. One of them believes that it leads to a Celestial City, the other that it leads nowhere; but since it is the only road there is, both must travel it. Neither has been this way before, and therefore neither is able to say what they will find around each next corner. During their journey they meet both with moments of refreshment and delight, and with moments of hardship and danger. All the time one of them thinks of her journey as a pilgrimage to the Celestial City, and interprets the pleasant parts as encouragements, and the obstacles as trials of her purpose and lessons in endurance, prepared by the sovereign of that city and designed to make of her a worthy citizen of the place when at last she arrives there. The other, however, believes none of this and sees their journey as an unavoidable and aimless ramble. Since he has no choice in the matter, he enjoys the good and endures the bad. But for him there is no Celestial City to be reached, no all-encompassing purpose ordaining their journey; only the road itself and the luck of the road in good weather and in bad.

During the course of the journey the issue between them is not an experimental one. They entertain different expectations not about the coming details of the road, but about its ultimate destination. And yet when they do turn the last corner it will be apparent that one of them has been right all the time and the other wrong. Thus although the issue between them has not been experimental it has nevertheless from the start been a real issue. They have not merely felt differently about the road; for one was feeling appropriately and the other inappropriately in relation to the actual state of affairs. Their opposed interpretations of the road constituted genuinely rival assertions, though assertions whose assertion-status has the peculiar characteristic of being guaranteed retrospectively by a future crux.[6]

There has been a good deal of discussion of this notion since it was first explicitly formulated in my *Faith and Knowledge* (1st edn) in 1957, and in an article, 'Theology and Verification', in 1960; and I want on this second time round to take account of this discussion.[7] I shall try to profit from those criticisms and suggestions which seem to me to be wholly or partly valid by restating the theory in a more acceptable way. For, whilst the basic conception seems to me to be sound, and indeed unavoidable, yet various clarifications, modifications and developments can I think usefully be made. Accordingly the present paper supplements rather than supplants the earlier one.

II

First a look back to the older discussions of verification. The attempts by the logical positivists to achieve a fully satisfactory verifiability criterion of factual meaningfulness never succeeded, and the quest for this elusive formula petered out at least a generation ago. But this does not mean that the insight or intuition which motivated the quest was illusory. On the contrary, the central core of the positivist contention seems undeniable. For it is simply the basic empiricist position that to exist, or to be the case, is to make a difference. That is to say, to assert that *x* exists is to assert an in-principle-observable difference between the actual universe and a possible universe which differs from it only in that the latter does not include *x*. That there is such a difference constitutes '*x* exists' a factual statement; and to observe those features of the universe which differentiate it from a possible *x*-less universe is to verify '*x* exists'. And, likewise, to assert *p* is to assert an in-principle-observable difference between the actual universe and a possible universe which differs from it only in that in the latter it is true that not-*p*. That there is such a difference constitutes *p* a factual statement; and to observe the features of the universe which differentiate it from a possible universe in which not-*p* is to verify *p*. Accordingly to say that *x* exists or that *p* is the case, but to deny that the existence of *x* or the truth of *p* makes any such in-principle-experienceable difference, would be to speak in a way that is pointless or meaningless. This, I would suggest, is the basic and non-controversial principle for which the logical positivists were contending. They contended for it within the framework of their own faith that established theories in the physical sciences are normative for all knowledge; and accordingly they assumed that the experienceable difference made by the truth of *p* must always be a difference of the kind that is registered in sense data.[8] Such a restrictive assumption was merely an *a priori* dogma. But, discounting this dogma, it is a perfectly good question to ask one who asserts that God exists, or that a divine purpose is being fulfilled in human life, what in-principle-experienceable difference it makes *whether* God exists or *whether* a divine purpose is being fulfilled in human life. We should therefore not allow ourselves to be tempted by Alvin Plantinga's short way with Flew's falsifiability challenge: 'In the light of ... the fact that it seems impossible to state the verifiability criterion, the question becomes acute: how *are* we to understand Flew's challenge? What exactly is he requiring of theological statements? Is he chiding the theist for ignoring some version of the verifiability criterion? If so, which version? Until these questions are answered it is impossible to determine whether his challenge is legitimate or even what the challenge *is*. If the notion of verifiability cannot so much as be explained, if we cannot so much as say what it is for a statement to be empirically verifiable, then we scarcely need worry about whether religious statements are or are not verifiable.'[9] Again, George Mavrodes, emphasising that no satisfactory verification criterion has yet been formulated, concludes that the attempt to point to possible situations which would confirm the truth of theism is misconceived.[10] These refusals to face the verifiability/falsifiability challenge strike me as examples of an unhelpful philosophical pedantry. For one does not have to have achieved a definitive formulation of a verifiability or falsifiability criterion to see that a supposedly declarative statement is pointless if it fails to claim that the facts of the universe are in some respect thus and not otherwise; and also that it is important for the theologian to be able to show that the central propositions with which he is concerned are *not* empty or pointless. Herbert Feigl's modest suggestion of 'confirmability-in-principle' as 'at least a *necessary* condition of factual meaningfulness', is surely entirely acceptable; and as Feigl himself pointed out, with particular reference to theology, it excludes only 'doctrines which are immune against tests of even the most indirect sort'.[11] I do not think that the theologian need be afraid of this basic principle of logical empiricism. Nor, incidentally, should he be afraid of the idea of 'testing' his beliefs: for testing, in this context, is not the sin of 'putting God to the test' but the true piety which waits patiently for the Lord to vindicate his faithful on the last day.

III

The idea of 'making an experienceable difference' covers the scale from complete and conclusive verifiability down through the various degrees of confirmability. At the top of this scale is the situation in which rational doubt as to the truth of p is entirely excluded; or (making explicit the role of the observer) in which doubt is entirely excluded from a rational observer's mind. Let us call this the point of cognitive conclusiveness. The nature of the doubt-excluding situation will of course differ according to the content of the proposition in question. That situation may be a simple or a complex state of affairs, depending upon the extent to which the difference made by the truth of p is specifically or variably defined, and the extent to which this difference is localised, or diffused in space or time or both. If the difference is sufficiently specific and local it will be capable of being observed in a single act of perception, which will then conclusively verify p. Let us call the characteristic of being capable of being verified by a single observation simple (as distinguished from complex) verifiability. For example, the difference made by there being a table in the next room can be registered by a single visual observation (perhaps supported by touching) so that 'There is a table in the next room' is close to exhibiting maximally simple verifiability. If on the other hand the difference made by the truth of p is variable in nature and/or diffused in extent, p may have to be confirmed by many cumulative observations. For example, 'John Smith is an honest man' cannot be verified by a single observation, for the experienceable difference made by his being an honest man is spread out over time and is also variable in the forms that it can take. The same is true of the theory of evolution, or indeed any large-scale scientific hypothesis. Let us describe these as having complex verifiability. In such cases there may be increasing confirmation until the point of cognitive conclusiveness is reached. This is the point at which rational doubt as to the truth of p has been entirely excluded and at which the concepts of confirmation and verification coincide.

This distinction between simple and complex verifiability enables us to avoid a wrong approach to the question of the verification of theistic statements. We should not ask, what single observation would verify them, but what development of our experience would progressively confirm them to the point at which there is no longer any room for rational doubt? For the existence of God is not a localised and therefore finite fact, comparable in this respect with the existence of a table in the next room, which can be verified by going into the next room and seeing and touching the table; and falsified by finding that there is no table there. The reality of God cannot be verified, analogously, by going to heaven and simply observing him there. For God is not one object or person among others in the heavenly world. As I pointed out in the 1960 article,

> God is described in Christian theology in terms of various absolute qualities, such as omnipotence, omnipresence, perfect goodness, infinite love, which cannot as such be observed by us, as can their finite analogues, limited power, local presence, finite goodness, and human love. One can recognize that a

being whom one 'encounters' has a given finite degree of power, but how does one recognize that he has unlimited power? How does one observe that an encountered being is *omni*potent? How does one perceive that his goodness and love, which one can perhaps see to exceed any human goodness and love, are actually infinite? Such qualities cannot be given in human experience.[12]

I would therefore suggest that the proposition whose eschatological verification we should consider is not 'God exists'; for this treats divine existence as an isolable and bounded fact. What we are seeking to verify is the truth of the theistic interpretation of the process of the universe, and this *verificandum* is embodied in a more complex proposition such as 'The theistic account of the character of the universe, and of what is taking place in its history, is true.' This proposition does not of course, and is not designed to, by-pass the question of the existence of God; for God must be referred to in giving an account of the meaning of 'theistic' in this context. God will appear in this account as the supreme being who controls the process of the universe and who is bringing it to the end which God intends. But the infinite nature of God's attributes – the infinity of God's power, knowledge, love, and so on – are not involved in this account. When the theist speaks, for example, of the power by which God rules the course of the universe, he or she believes, and is assuming, the infinity of that power; but this infinity is not in fact exercised in relation to the finite realm which is the field of human cognition. The degree of divine power exercised in relation to the universe as it is experienced and to be experienced by human beings is a power sufficient to fulfil God's purposes for the creation; but it is not, strictly speaking, infinite power. And the same principle applies to the other divine attributes. The Deity is believed by Christians to be infinite; and we must inquire presently concerning the grounds of this belief. But God's alleged impingement upon the creation, raising the question whether its character as a divinely ruled process might be capable of confirmation or verification, is necessarily a finite impingement: power exerted non-destructively upon a finite object must itself be finite.

Thus an eschatological situation which is to verify the truth of the theistic account of the universe and of what is taking place in it

will not have the impossible task of verifying the infinite nature of
God's attributes, but the more limited task of confirming to the
full that the history of the universe has led to an end-state in which
the postulated divine purpose for humanity can be seen to be
fulfilled. The assertion that is to be verified is thus an assertion
about what is going on in human existence and its environment.
The theistic claim is that what is going on is the gradual creation
of perfected finite persons who are eventually to live in unimpeded
communion with God. The religious ambivalence of the present
world, including its characteristic mixture of good and evil, sets us
at an epistemic distance from God which leaves room for further
confirmation, whilst at the same time making possible a free
response of faith to God. But – it is claimed – as we approach perfection we will become increasingly open to and conscious of God
in environments in which the ambiguities of this life will have
been left behind and in which the divine goodness and love will be
increasingly evident. Thus the movement towards the end-state
involves a gradual transformation of the individual in the course
of that person's transition – no doubt through various intermediate environments – to the final unambiguous situation which is
traditionally symbolised as heaven. This situation will be religiously unambiguous in the following sense: in the present world
men and women believe in the reality of God on the basis of a
religious experience which is a (putative) consciousness of living
in the divine presence. Some aspects of the world manifestly
cohere with and thus support this belief whilst others do not. All
that is good, beautiful, creative and uplifting in the world process
agrees with and thus far confirms the belief in a good and loving
creator, whilst pain and suffering, wickedness and ugliness are
dissonant circumstances which thus far disconfirm that belief. I
have argued elsewhere that it is rational for the religious person
now, in this life, experiencing the world process with its mixture of
good and evil as taking place in the presence and according to the
purpose of God, to believe with full subjective certainty in the
reality of God.[13] But this does not mean that his or her faith,
rational though it is, is not capable of further and fuller
confirmation as the creative process increasingly unfolds towards
its completion in the eschatological state.[14] In that state one's
God-consciousness will be at a maximum. One will be continuously aware of living in the divine presence; and that
awareness will no longer be in tension with the circumstances of

sin and suffering, ugliness and deprivation, which at present leave room for rational doubt. We are contemplating an experience of progressive sanctification (not, incidentally, embodied in the original parable of the journey) accompanied by an increasingly powerful and pervasive sense of existing in the presence of an invisible transcendent power who knows us, who loves us, and who can be seen to be drawing us towards a perfection in which we are to dwell in joyous communion with that transcendent reality. I suggest that this would constitute mounting and increasingly massive confirmation of theistic faith; and that the completion of the process in the endless life of the 'kingdom of God' would constitute a situation of cognitive conclusiveness in which there would be no room for rational doubt concerning the truth of the religious understanding of human existence, or concerning the reality of the divine being, awareness of whom is the central characteristic of the eschatological situation.

It will be of interest to some at least that the last book of the Bible contains a picture of the eschaton which largely accords with this hypothesis. The life of heaven is to be the life of a community inhabiting a city. God is not a visible object there, but nevertheless will be intimately present to the community of the redeemed; for 'Behold, the dwelling of God is with men. He will dwell with them, and they shall be his people' (Revelation 21.3). The new heaven and earth are to be free from evil; for God 'will wipe away every tear from their eyes, and death shall be no more, neither shall there be mourning nor crying nor pain any more' (v. 4). Men and women will be so totally conscious of God that there will be no need of a temple. They will be living all the time in the temple of the divine presence: for the city's 'temple is the Lord God Almighty and the Lamb' (v. 22).

IV

But, it may perhaps be objected, in this eschatological situation God will still be no more available to human observation, or God's existence verified, than now. Human beings will still be expected to believe in a God whom they cannot see. How then can theistic belief be said to have been verified? The answer is, I think, implicit in what has already been proposed. The redeemed (whom I assume ultimately to include everyone – though this is of course a theological rather than a philosophical opinion) will have experienced in this world, or will have come to experience at some stage between this world and the final heavenly state, what they take to be an awareness of existing in the presence of God and of being freely led within the divine providence towards the fulfilment of their human potentialities in the community of humanity perfected. In experiencing their life in this way, and in believing in accordance with their experience, they believe in the reality of God and in the process of the universe as God's creative work. And this belief is progressively confirmed and then verified in the experience of moving towards and then participating in the eschatological situation of a perfected human community in which the consciousness of God's presence is universally shared.

But, let us now ask, might not a group of hard-boiled atheists arrive in the eschatological world and persist in holding to a naturalistic interpretation of all that is going on? And does not this possibility show that what I have been calling eschatological verification should really be called eschatological faith? There are two replies to be made to this suggestion. First, there is indeed a sense in which all cognition, involving as it does an element of interpretation, can be said to involve faith. The idea of verification trades upon the difference between interpretation in circumstances which leave room for rational doubt as to the truth of the interpretation, and interpretation in circumstances which leave no such room. And the notion of heaven is that of a situation which excludes rational doubt concerning the truth of the theistic interpretation. But heavenly cognition, like earthly cognition, will still involve the element of interpretation which I for one wish to identify with faith. However, second, the picture of a squad of atheists arriving in heaven is precluded by the hypothesis that we reach the eschatological world by fulfilling the God-given potentialities of our nature, including the potentiality for full God-consciousness. There can therefore be no atheists in heaven. If the theological opinion is correct that all people without exception will eventually attain to full God-consciousness, then the reason why there are no atheists in heaven will be that in the end there are no atheists: every former atheist will in the course of his or her personal history in the realms between this and the heavenly world have become a theist. If on the other hand this universalist opinion is mistaken, then the reason why there are no atheists in heaven will be that so long as one remains an atheist one is not in heaven; for heaven is the final state of perfect communion between God and God's creatures.

But, granting that all the citizens of heaven will be continuously conscious of existing in God's presence, can we not nevertheless still ask whether they may not be in a state of delusion? They may have what they take to be a vivid awareness of the divine presence; and it may be entirely reasonable for them, on the basis of this experience, to believe unquestioningly in the reality of God and to go on for ever experiencing in this way and being utterly convinced of God's reality. But may they not nevertheless be being eternally hallucinated? Is not this still a logical possibility; and must we not therefore conclude that the question of God's existence will still not have been definitively settled?

Here we encounter the old and much discussed notion of unappeasable scepticism. For perpetual scepticism in relation to an eternally coherent theistic experience of heaven would raise the same issues as perpetual scepticism in relation to the reality of our present physical environment and of other persons. Although the question is highly debatable, I accept solipsism as a logical possibility. It seems to me logically possible that the world in which I am living, and the other people with whom I suppose myself to be jointly inhabiting it, exist only as modifications of my own consciousness, and that I am the only consciousness there is. In that case my continued coherent experience of an external environment and of other people existing independently of myself fail to constitute contrary evidence, since the 'evidence' itself exists only in my own mind. But, together with many philosophers today, whilst acknowledging the logical possibility of such unappeasable scepticism I simply reject it as insane. And I would suggest that it would be at least equally insane to invoke this kind of scepticism in relation to an endlessly continued experience of heaven.

But what about the infinite divine attributes, consideration of which was postponed earlier in the discussion? I have acknowledged that even in an eschatological life lived in unimpeded consciousness of God's presence we cannot expect to experience the infinity of the divine being. This is not to say that we shall experience the presence of a finite deity, but that we shall experience the presence of a deity who indefinitely exceeds ourselves, but whose infinity can nevertheless not be given within the confines of human experience. That God is infinite, and has the divine properties in an infinite mode, is a conclusion of natural theology. I think there are good arguments in natural theology for this conclusion, though it would be too large an extension of the discussion to examine them here. The point at the moment is that the reality of God, defined as infinite, is not verifiable within human experience, although the reality of an indefinitely great God, whom we may believe on the basis of philosophical reasoning to be infinite, is in principle confirmable to the point of cognitive conclusiveness.

There is however also available to us the answer offered in my 1960 article, namely that the infinity of God is a revealed truth, believed on the authority of a teacher, namely Christ, whose veracity will be confirmed in the eschatological situation:

> Our beliefs about God's infinite being are not capable of observational verification, being beyond the scope of human experience, but they are susceptible of indirect verification by the removal of rational doubt concerning the authority of Christ. An experience of the reign of the Son in the Kingdom of the Father would confirm that authority, and therewith, indirectly, the validity of Jesus' teaching concerning the character of God in his infinite transcendent nature.[15]

However I now see two difficulties in this response. One arises from a concern not to restrict the discussion within exclusively Christian boundaries. No longer thinking of Jesus as the one and only revelation of God, I do not want to treat his teaching as our sole source of knowledge of God's nature. But another related difficulty is that it is far from clear that Jesus did in fact teach that God is infinite. He lived in close and intimate awareness of God, dwelling consciously in the heavenly Father's unseen presence and giving himself wholly to serve the divine purposes on earth; but we do not seem to have any evidence that he had occasion to raise the question of God's infinity. In general, the experience of God as a personal presence to whom one speaks in prayer is an experience in the finite mode; and, if the thought of God as infinite is associated with it, this has been imported from some other source – probably the natural theology embodied in one's religious tradition.

One can perhaps best express this theologically by saying that God as infinite transcends existence: God *is* but does not exist. But

God as related to the world – in Pascal's phrase 'the God of
Abraham, of Isaac and of Jacob' in distinction from the God of the
philosophers – does exist.

V

The question has been raised whether the experiences which are
supposed to verify theism are theistic or non-theistic experiences.[16] On the one hand, it is said, if the supposedly verifying
experiences are non-theistic ones – such as hearing a voice – they
can never verify a religious belief; for no number of nontheological facts can add up to a theological fact. But if on the
other hand the verifying experiences are religious experiences –
such as hearing *God's* voice – then the argument runs in a circle;
for we still need a further verification that the voice is indeed
God's voice. Any proffered verification of this will consist either in
a non-theistic experience (which, being non-theistic, can never do
the job) or in a theistic experience – which will again require a
further verification of *its* theistic character; and then the same
question will arise about that experience, and so on *ad infinitum*.

But rather than worry about how to get out of this predicament
we can avoid getting into it. We should begin, I would suggest,
where the present essay began: with the fact that some people
experience the events of their lives and of the world theistically –
that is, in terms of the concept of God.[17] All conscious experience
of our environment is in terms of the concepts by which we
apprehend (or of course misapprehend) objects and situations as
having this or that character or meaning. In other words, all
experiencing is, as I have argued elsewhere,[18] experiencing-as.
The (theistically) religious mind experiences life as being lived in
the unseen presence of God and within the sphere of an on-going
divine purpose. That some people have experienced and that
some do experience in this way is an historical fact: the Bible is
largely an anthology of first-hand reports of this mode of
experiencing-as, and there are contemporary believers who
experience in essentially the same way. The question, then, is
whether the theistic conviction which, as I have said above, arises
from and feeds into this way of experiencing, will be confirmed by
the individual's further, including post-mortem, experiences; and
whether it will be confirmed to the point of cognitive conclusive-

ness which we call verification. The eschatological religions, at least, claim that this will in fact happen; and I have been arguing that this claim gives factual-assertion status to their systems of beliefs.

It should be added that in principle such verification could occur in *this* world also. The world could conceivably change into a 'heaven on earth' in which perfect human beings live in a full God-consciousness unimpeded by any jarring circumstances. But, although there have been strands of teaching predicting something like this, both in messianic Judaism and in millenarian Christianity, yet the larger tradition of the theistic religions is the one which the notion of eschatological verification brings to bear upon the logic of religious language. It should perhaps be stressed again that 'eschatological verification' is not a desperate *ad hoc* device invented to meet a sceptical challenge but draws out that aspect of the traditional theistic system of belief which establishes that system as a complex factual assertion.

Some have seen it as a fatal flaw in the theory of eschatological verification that it rests upon belief in continued human existence after death. For this belief seems to them a fantastic fairy-tale, not to be taken seriously. Here I can only say that the Christian understanding of the universe includes belief in life after death as an indispensable component and that if that belief could be proved to be false Christian theism (though not every kind of theism) would thereby be falsified. For the 'life everlasting' is in my view one of the essential claims by which Christian theism stands or falls; and that there are such cruxes is of course the nub of the theistic response to the verification/falsification challenge.

It is in relation to this idea of human survival of death that the verifiability/falsifiability asymmetry noted in my 1960 article arises. That is to say, the prediction that I shall, after my bodily death, be conscious, continue to undergo new experiences, and have memories of my death and of my life before and after it, is a prediction which will be conclusively verified in my own experience if it is true but which will not be falsified in my own experience if it is false. However it does not follow from this that theism is necessarily unfalsifiable-if-false. This depends upon the actual nature of the universe, given that theism is false. If materialistic naturalism is true and human beings perish totally at death, then theism would not be falsifiable – unless, again, it could be *proved* that we perish totally at death, in which case this proof would at the same time serve to falsify theism. But, as another possibility, the facts of the universe could be such that theism will eventually be definitively seen to be false – as has been argued by Gregory Kavka in terms of the obverse of the kind of post-mortem situation which would verify theism, namely a universe unendingly dominated by an evil power.[19] There is, then, the following partial asymmetry between the verifiability and the falsifiability of Christian theism. If Christian theism is true, its truth will be confirmed within future human experience to the point of cognitive conclusiveness; but if it is false its falsity may or may not be conclusively established in future human experience, depending upon the actual non-theistic character of the universe.

POSTSCRIPT

What is the relation between religious pluralism and this concept of eschatological verification?

I have presented the idea here in theistic, and indeed Christian, terms. But it could also be stated in Jewish, in Muslim or in theistic Hindu terms. Again, it could be presented in non-theistic terms, depicting the end state as conceived in advaitic Hindu or in the various schools of Buddhist thought. From the point of view of the theory of the humanly conditioned *personae* and *impersonae* of the Real outlined in Chapter 3, and of the eschatological theory to be outlined in Chapter 9, it seems likely that the different expectations cherished within the different traditions will ultimately turn out to be partly correct and partly incorrect. It could be that in a mind-dependent *bardo* phase immediately after death (see below, pp. 141–2) these expectations will be fulfilled in the experience of believers – Christians, Hindus, Muslims, and so on each encountering what their different traditions have taught them to anticipate. But as they advance beyond that phase and the process of ego-transcendence continues, their pictures of the universe, and their expectations concerning its future development, will themselves develop, becoming gradually more adequate to the reality. And within the long span of this development it may well be that the final state will prove to be beyond the horizon of our present powers of imagination.

Thus the long-term development of the universe and of human existence as part of it may be other than any of our earthly religious traditions anticipate. From this more comprehensive point of view the question is not whether the truth of a Christian, or a Muslim, or a Hindu, or a Buddhist interpretation is ultimately verifiable within human experience but whether the truth of a religious as opposed to a naturalistic interpretation of the universe is ultimately capable of being verified. The answer is 'Yes'. For, if there is a further development of human experience, beyond this present life, which is incompatible with a naturalistic understanding of the universe but which develops and enlarges our various religious understandings of it, this will constitute verification of the religious side of the religious/naturalistic opposition.

And so the principle of eschatological verification is highly relevant to the question of the basically factual character of religious understandings of the universe, and to the ultimate resolution of the debate between religious and naturalistic (including atheistic) believers. It is probably not, however, directly relevant to the assessment of the conflicting truth-claims of the various traditions. (This latter point is discussed briefly above, pp. 99–100.)

NOTES

1. Richard M. Hare, 'Theology and Falsification' in *New Essays in Philosophical Theology*, ed. Antony Flew and Alasdair MacIntyre (London: SCM; New York: Macmillan, 1955). Repr. in numerous places.
2. Antony Flew, 'Theology and Falsification', ibid.
3. R. B. Braithwaite, *An Empiricist's View of the Nature of Religious Belief* (Cambridge and New York: Cambridge University Press, 1955). Repr. in numerous places.
4. Basil Mitchell, 'Theology and Falsification', in *New Essays*. Cf. Mitchell's *The Justification of Religious Belief* (London: Macmillan; New York: Seabury Press, 1973) ch. 1.
5. Ian Crombie, in 'Theology and Falsification', ibid.
6. John Hick, 'Theology and Verification', *Theology Today*, vol. xvii (1960) pp. 18–19. Repr. in numerous places, such as *The Logic of God: Theology and Verification*, ed. Malcolm L. Diamond and Thomas V. Litzenburg (Indianapolis: Bobbs-Merrill, 1975).
7. W. Bean, 'Eschatological Verification: Fortress or Fairyland?', *Methodos* vol. xvi, no. 62 (1964); William T. Blackstone, *The Problem of Religious Knowledge* (Englewood Cliffs, NJ: Prentice-Hall, 1963) ch. 7; Carl-Reinhold Brakenheilm, *How Philosophy Shapes Theories of Religion: An Analysis of Contemporary Philosophies of Religion with Special Regard to the Thought of John*

Wilson, John Hick and D. Z. Phillips (Lund: Gleerup, 1975) ch. 3; William H. Brenner, 'Faith and Experience: A Critical Study of John Hick's Contribution to the Philosophy of Religion' (unpublished doctoral dissertation, University of Virginia, 1970) ch. 4; James I. Campbell, *The Language of Religion* (New York: Bruce, 1971) ch. 4; Edward Cell, *Language, Existence and God* (New York: Abingdon Press, 1971) ch. 8; Stephen T. Davis, 'Theology, Verification, and Falsification', *International Journal for Philosophy of Religion*, vol. VI, no. 1 (1975); Peter Donovan, *Religious Language* (London: Sheldon Press, 1976) ch. 7; D. R. Duff-Forbes, 'Theology and Falsification Again', *Australasian Journal of Theology*, vol. XXXIX (1961); Rem B. Edwards, *Religion and Reason* (New York: Harcourt Brace Jovanovich, 1972) ch. 14; Gregory S. Kavka, 'Eschatological Falsification', *Religious Studies*, vol. XII, no. 2 (1976); Kenneth H. Klein, *Positivism and Christianity: A Study of Theism and Verifiability* (The Hague: Martinus Nijhoff, 1974) ch. 4; George I. Mavrodes, 'God and Verification', *Canadian Journal of Theology*, vol. XIX (1964); James Alfred Martin, *The New Dialogue between Philosophy and Theology* (New York: Seabury Press, and London: A. & C. Black, 1966) ch. 3; Basil Mitchell, *The Justification of Religious Belief* (London: Macmillan; New York: Seabury Press, 1973) ch. 1; Kai Nielsen, 'Eschatological Verification', *Canadian Journal of Theology*, vol. IX (1963), repr. in *The Logic of God*. Kai Nielsen, *Contemporary Critiques of Religion* (London: Macmillan; New York: Herder and Herder, 1971) ch. 4; Terence Penelhum, *Problems of Religious Knowledge* (London: Macmillan; New York: Herder and Herder, 1971) ch. 4, and *Religion and Rationality* (New York: Random House, 1971) ch. 11; H. H. Price, *Belief* (London: George Allen and Unwin; New York: Humanities Press, 1969) ser. II, lecture 10; Paul F. Schmidt, *Religious Knowledge* (Glencoe, NY: The Free Press, 1961) ch. 4; Michael Tooley, 'John Hick and the Concept of Eschatological Verification', *Religious Studies*, vol. XII, no. 2 (1976); Keith E. Yandell, *Basic Issues in the Philosophy of Religion* (Boston: Allyn and Bacon, 1971) ch. 6.

8. In his article 'John Hick and the Concept of Eschatological Verification' (*Religious Studies*, vol. XII), Michael Tooley speaks of 'the verifiability principle' as though there were a single such criterion available to be applied to theology. He seems to be taking his stand somewhere back in the 1930s. From this position he argues that the existence of persons, both human and divine, as 'experientially transcendent entities' is in principle unverifiable and therefore that the theory of eschatological verification fails. He claims that, 'given the verifiability principle, there is a very plausible argument which demonstrates that no factual meaning can be assigned to talk about experientially transcendent entities' (p. 198), whether human or divine. I would agree that a conception of verification which is so restrictive as to exclude statements about human persons will also exclude statements about God. However Tooley has himself elsewhere argued, surely rightly, that such a concept of verification is untenable ('Theological Statements and the Question of an Empiricist Criterion of Cognitive Significance', in *The Logic of God*). It is because I also take this view that in both my 1960 article and in the present essay I have defined verifiability more broadly, in terms of removal of grounds for rational doubt.

9. Alvin Plantinga, *God and Other Minds* (Ithaca, NY: Cornell University Press, 1967) p. 168.
10. George Mavrodes, 'God and Verification', *Canadian Journal of Theology*, vol. x (1964), repr. in *The Logic of God*.
11. Herbert Feigl, 'Some Major Issues and Developments in the Philosophy of Science of Logical Empiricism', *Minnesota Studies in the Philosophy of Science*, vol. i (Minneapolis: University of Minnesota Press, 1956) p. 15.
12. Hick, 'Theology and Verification', *Theology Today*, vol. xvii, p. 28.
13. John Hick, *Faith and Knowledge*, 2nd edn (Ithaca, NY: Cornell University Press, 1966; and London: Macmillan, 1967) ch. 9, and *Arguments for the Existence of God* (London: Macmillan, 1970; and New York: Herder and Herder, 1971) ch. 7.
14. Michael Tooley says, 'If Hick is claiming both that religious people now have experiences which provide them with knowledge, or at least warranted belief, about the existence of God, and that theological statements can be shown to be verifiable, and hence factually significant, only by appealing to the possibility of certain experiences after death, his overall position would seem to be inconsistent' (*Religious Studies*, vol. xii, no. 2, p. 182). But surely there is no inconsistency here. There is a present belief, based on present religious experience, in the reality of God; and there is the philosophical question whether, under a reasonable verifiability criterion, this is a genuinely factual belief; to which the answer is that it is part of a system or organism of beliefs which includes verifiable eschatological expectations. These expectations ensure that what seems to the believer to be an affirmation of existence is not, in reality, merely a factually contentless *blik*.
15. Hick, 'Theology and Verification', *Theology Today*, vol. xvii, p. 29.
16. Kai Nielsen based his main critique of the theory of eschatological verification on the premise that the verification of a religious belief must be in non-religious terms ('Eschatological Verification', *Canadian Journal of Theology*, vol. ix), and Michael Tooley in his recent article likewise assumes that 'the description of the experiences that verify any statement should ultimately be couched in purely observational terms' (*Religious Studies*, vol. xii, no. 2 p. 189), by which in this case he means 'purely nontheological terms' (p. 190). This seems to me fundamentally mistaken. The verification of a factual statement must be in terms of *experience*; but not only is human experience not confined to the registering of bare sense-data, but it is even doubtful whether it ever takes this form. Here Tooley is again taking us back to the 1930s.
17. Michael Tooley asks, 'could a person understand what experiences Hick has in mind here [referring to the eschatological situation] if he did not understand theological language? If not, reference to these purportedly verifying experiences will not explain the meaning of theological statements to one who does not already understand them' (ibid., p. 188). However I have not suggested that the eschatological situation will explain the meaning of theological statements to one who does not already understand them. I begin from the fact that there is already, in this present life, a putative awareness of God, expressed in religious statements which the religious believer understands. (This is not of course to say that anyone ever wholly understands God.) These statements are part of a unitary body of beliefs

which include eschatological beliefs, and it is these latter that give factual-assertion status to the system as a whole.

18. John Hick, 'Religious Faith as Experiencing-as' in *Talk of God*, ed. Godfrey Vesey (London: Macmillan; New York: St Martin's Press, 1969). Repr. in John Hick, *God and the Universe of Faiths* (London: Macmillan; New York: St Martin's Press, 1973), and elsewhere. Cf. also Chapter 2 above.

19. Kavka, 'Eschatological Falsification', *Religious Studies*, vol. xii, no. 2.

9   Present and Future Life*

It is a curious feature of the present time that a boom in secular interest in the idea of a life after death seems to be matched by a recession in high-level theological interest in that possibility. There is today a wave of popular non-religious concern about death and about a post-mortem existence, expressed in para-psychology, occultism, thanatology, and talk of mediumship, reincarnation, out-of-the-body experiences and the reports of those who have been revived after having been clinically dead. And yet at the same time some of the best Christian thinking today is inclined to de-emphasise the idea of the life to come, even to the point of virtually abandoning it as an element in the Christian message. It is true that there is much talk of the future (sometimes with a capital F), and of Christian hope and of the radically eschatological character of the Gospel. For example, Jürgen Moltmann has said that 'From first to last, and not merely in the epilogue, Christianity is eschatology, is hope, forward looking and forward moving . . . .'[1] But when we read on we find that the hope of which he speaks is, in so far as it has any content, a this-worldly hope and that 'the life everlasting' has been reduced to a penumbra of mythic imagery. Again, Wolfhart Pannenberg has said that 'eschatology is no longer a marginal problem of theology, which one could leave to the last chapter of dogmatics, but the basis upon which everything in Christian tradition is built';[2] and he has spoken of God in eschatological terms as 'the absolute future'. However we find that the life beyond death of which he speaks is not really a future life at all but our past life seen again in a new light. To summarise in this way the eschatologies of these two distinguished thinkers does not of course do justice to their thought, but merely serves as a reminder of one aspect of it. I have discussed this aspect more fully

* The 1977 Ingersoll Lecture on Immortality, delivered at Harvard University, and reprinted with permission from the *Harvard Theological Review*, vol. LXXI, no. 1–2 (January–April 1978).

elsewhere.[3] My point at the moment is simply that the current vogue of high eschatological language does not centre upon or even necessarily entail the idea of a life beyond death. And, whilst Christian thought is today very various, so that no characterisation will apply right across the board, yet it can I think be said that among many of our more thoughtful theological contemporaries there is a feeling that talk of an after-life is not only too improbable factually, but also too morally and religiously dubious, to constitute a proper branch of Christian belief.

My purpose in this lecture is to oppose this view – highly though I respect those who hold it.

Let me then proceed immediately to take up the two main considerations which, if I hear them aright, have led many theologians today to de-emphasise that element of the Christian tradition referred to in the creed as 'the life everlasting'. One is that the doctrine is unbelievable to the modern mind; and the other, that it rests upon a kind of self-concern from which true religion should have freed us. I think that some are particularly moved by one of these considerations, some by the other, and others again by both.

Let us confront first the widespread view that belief in a post-mortem life is no longer a rational possibility for the inhabitants of our science-oriented twentieth century thought-world. Here the human being is prevailingly seen as an animal that has evolved a large and marvellously complex brain in virtue of which it has not only survived and multiplied but has created an inner environment of ideas expressed in a rich outer fabric of cultural forms. Consciousness, which is the 'space' of this inner world, is held to be a reflexive functioning of the brain, so that the entire mental life, conscious and unconscious, either consists in or is an epiphenomenal reflection of a patterned process of cerebral events. There is in fact no important difference, from the point of view of the question of the continuation of personal life after bodily death, between the older epiphenomenalism and the more recent mind–brain identity theory. According to the latter, electro-chemical accounts of neural events and psychological accounts of mental events are alternative descriptions of the same thing, which is the functioning of the brain. And, according to the older variation, conscious experience is a secondary by-product of a cerebral history, so that mental events are produced by brain events but never *vice versa*. Accordingly, mental episodes such as thinking and willing cannot cause their corresponding brain occurrences but simply reflect existing brain activity. On either view the unique stream of images and feelings and of intellectual and volitional activities constituting a personal self-consciousness must inevitably terminate as the brain ceases to function. Hence, any notion of the conscious personality persisting after the death of the physical organism can only be a fantasy. Such fantasies are generated, presumably, by the complexity of cortical connections which the brain has developed beyond the requirement of immediate biological needs, a surplus capacity whose play gives rise to humanity's religions, art, literature, philosophy – and also, presumably, science.

So far as its implications for eschatology are concerned, this naturalistic view of the human being has been accepted by a number of our leading theologians today. Let me cite briefly two representative figures, one from Europe and the other from the United States. Wolfhart Pannenberg says that modern anthropology 'removes the basis for the idea of immortality of the soul';[4] and again, that the 'concept of the undying continuation of the soul while the body perishes has become untenable today'.[5] And Gordon Kaufman says that

> Men of other ages and cultures, subscribing to different psychologies, could develop doctrines of the 'immortality of the soul' according to which man's true essence is divine and survives bodily death; to modern psychology and medicine, man appears as a psychosomatic unity whose spiritual life is inseparably bound to its physical base. The end of the body, therefore, is the end of the man . . . .[6]

And I think you will agree that these statements can be matched from the writings of a number of other theologians on both sides of the Atlantic.

This unqualified rejection by some of our foremost Christian thinkers of the dualist view of the human person as ontologically other than the functioning of one's physical brain is, I believe, at best very premature and at worst a disastrous mistake. Let me remind you of some of the main unresolved points of doubt and debate concerning mind–brain identity. The first is that it is a theory which tends to be taken for granted within a general naturalistic horizon of thought, but not a conclusion established by any of the special sciences, and certainly not by brain research. Indeed it has been rejected in favour of mind–brain dualism by some of the leaders in this field. Second, the mind–brain identity theory involves deep philosophical problems, which are also shared by epiphenomenalism. One of these is the paradox that if the mind is either identical with or a reflection of the physical functioning of the brain, whilst this is itself an integral part of the system of nature, then believing, judging, proving, inferring, and so on are, or are reflections of, causally determined physical events. To claim that this is the status of your own beliefs and reasonings (including of course your belief about the nature of mental activity) is to present them as having the significance only of causally necessitated physical events. Thus belief in the truth of the mind–brain identity or of the epiphenomenalist theory is a belief which categorises itself as either identical with or as the reflection of a causally determined physical process. But, having concluded that one's conclusions represent the causally deter-mined state of a particular portion of matter, one has undermined one's preference for the state of one's own lump of grey matter rather than for that of another lump of grey matter which has come to a different conclusion. Third, some of the evidence of parapsychology – particularly the evidence for interactions, not mediated by physical signals, between one stream of conscious-ness and another – is extremely hard to fit into the mind–brain identity or epiphenomenalist theories.

I am not going to develop these three points here. I mention them simply as a reminder that, regardless of any theological implications, the naturalistic view of mind as either identical with or as wholly dependent upon and determined by brain is debatable and debated, alike as scientific hypothesis and as philosophical theory. But from a theological point of view there is also the problem that the idea of God is already the idea of disembodied consciousness. All schools of Christian thought are agreed that, whatever more we may mean by 'God', we at least mean unlimited personal consciousness and, further, that the divine consciousness is neither produced by, dependent upon, nor identical with a physical brain. A theologian who postulates a divine consciousness without physical basis has thus already moved irrevocably beyond the naturalistic horizon; and for such a one to declare impossible a non-material human mind after affirming the non-material divine mind is to strain out a gnat after swallowing a camel!

But the view of the human being as an indissoluble psycho-physical unity is generally applied by these theologians specifically against the idea of the immortality of the soul, in distinction from the alternative idea of the resurrection of the body, which they see as more acceptable. And it is true that if you adopt the view of the human creature as a purely bodily being, but reject much of the wider naturalistic world-view of which this is today a part, you can then switch from 'Hellenic immortality' to 'Hebraic resurrection' without depriving your theology of its eschatological fulfilment. However, this move will not admit you into the cultural world from which a belief in the mind's survival of bodily death would have excluded you. For within that cultural world resurrection is as fantastic as immortality. Leaving aside the totally unbelievable notion of the coming forth of corpses from their graves, a realistic conception of resurrection would have to postulate the divine re-creation of psycho-physical beings in another world or worlds. More about this later. But note at the moment that it lies as far outside our contemporary naturalistic horizon as does the mind's survival of the death of the body. It is true that resurrection in this sense is not in fact ruled out by any established conclusions in any of the special sciences, any more than is the survival of consciousness after bodily death; but it *is* ruled out by the assumptions and habits of judgement operating within a science-based culture. And therefore, if one has abandoned the idea of the survival of the mind because of its rejection by this culture, it would be consistent to reject the idea of resurrection also for the same reason.

Let me now take stock and then move on. I have pointed out that there is a long-standing debate amongst scientists and philosophers about the status of mental life. This debate is at present open and could go either way; or it could indeed prove to be a perpetual debate, never destined to be definitively settled within either science or philosophy. In this situation it seems to me odd that many theologians should so readily adopt a monistic theory, whether in the form of epiphenomenalism or of mind–brain identity. For their own starting-point as theologians is the existence of divine mind prior to and independent of matter. I do not say that these two positions are totally irreconcilable; for there could in principle be non-embodied divine mind but no non-embodied creaturely minds. But I nevertheless wonder why theologians should be so quick to opt for a mind-brain identity or an epiphenomenalist theory which is not only unproved but which also generates profound philosophical and theological problems. If their concern is to avoid contradicting contemporary secular assumptions, I fear that they have set themselves an impossible task. For when, having renounced the mind's survival of bodily death, they go on to speak of resurrection and of a divine re-creation of the psychophysical person, they transgress the limits set by our science-oriented culture quite as flagrantly as if they had asserted the immortality of the soul.

But now let us turn to a more profound consideration which has led many theologians today, and indeed often the same ones, to de-emphasise the Christian doctrine of the life to come. This is the thought that the doctrine is morally or spiritually harmful. It has of course always been regarded by Marxists as the opium of the people, a drug which reconciles the downtrodden masses to their unjust lot by filling their imaginations with a heavenly paradise to come. And there certainly have been periods in the history of many societies in which the idea of a future life has been exploited as an instrument of social control. I should guess that those days are now over, even in the most backward countries; and certainly they are long since over so far as the United States and Europe are concerned. But the idea which influences a number of contemporary theologians centres upon the individual rather than the community. It is that the concern for personal immortality (whether by the resurrection of the body or the immortality of the soul) is a selfish and thus a basically irreligious concern. It is a concern for the perpetuation of the little ego. The beloved 'I' wants to live for ever; it cannot bear the thought that the universe should some day go on without it. And there is indeed something profoundly unbecoming in the spectacle of the average grubby little human ego demanding to be immortalised. I am sure that those who emphasise this, and who accordingly have qualms about the widespread desire for personal immortality, are thus far right. But I do not think that they are right in going on to conclude that the doctrine of a future life is mistaken. Rather, I would suggest, their insight is in harmony with the deeper teaching of the great world religions – in the context of which, however, it is not inimical to the idea of a life or lives to come but on the contrary requires this. Let me then remind you of three great themes which are common, in different forms, to the major religious traditions.

The first is that of the immense potentialities of the human spirit. From a naturalistic or humanist standpoint one can speculate about the further evolutionary possibilities of the human species. Future forms of *homo sapiens*, thousands or millions of years hence, may be more intelligent, more morally mature, and more successful in organising their social life than humanity today. But, if there are in fact to be such developments, we today cannot know of them or participate in them. We can at best be related to such people of the future as means to an end. But the great world religions, without being concerned to assert or deny the possibility of such developments, affirm the value of the present individual not merely as a means to a further end but as already an end. They say to each human being: *you* are a child of God, made in the divine image and loved by God, and you can begin now to experience the new life in conscious relationship to God; or *you* are a potential Buddha, and can attain the liberation which is *nirvāṇa*; or *you* are in the depths of your being one with Brahman and can become *jivanmukti*, a liberated soul whilst still on this earth. Thus the message of the religions is not only for men and women of the remote future but for each living man and woman now. Further, the immense potentialities of human existence, which give the religious message the quality of a gospel, are not restricted (except in some extreme double-predestinarian dogmas) to any section or period of humanity but are affirmed of *all* human beings. And when we look at the lives of the saints and. hear of the experiences of the mystics of the different traditions we see revealed aspects of the human potential which have yet to be realised in ourselves. In Christianity we sometimes express this by saying that we see in the life of Jesus the perfection of the human nature that he shared with us. And salvation, or liberation, or entry into eternal life, means fulfilling this potentiality in relationship with the divine Reality known as infinite love, or known as *Satchitananda* (infinite being–consciousness–happiness), or known as the eternal cosmic Buddha. This, then, is the first of the religious themes to which I want to draw attention: the message, addressed to every individual, of the illimitably better possibility to which every human creature is heir.

Moving now to a second theme, the great world faiths also teach that the realising of the deeper human potential is a matter not of perpetuating but rather of transcending our present self-enclosed individual existence. The little ego is challenged to self-renunciation and the overcoming of egoity in the larger corporate life of perfected humanity. Thus in Jesus's teaching we are called to love others as much as we love ourselves, to give and forgive without limit, not to retaliate but to live a life of other-regarding love. One who responds fully to this call has ceased to be a self-seeking ego and has become a channel of the divine grace and love. And in the later Christian tradition the mystics were to speak of the way of 'self-naughting' and even sometimes of the eventual absorption of the creature within the divine life. The other Semitic faiths, Judaism and Islam, call in the one case for a life of complete obedience to the divine Torah, and in the other for a total submission of the human ego to the will of Allah. The great Eastern religions of Hinduism and Buddhism both teach that separate egoity is ultimately false, although it can sustain its false existence through innumerable psycho-physical lives until at last the point is reached of readiness to lose oneself in the infinite being–consciousness–happiness of Brahman, or in the infinite mystery of *nirvāṇa*. Thus in each case, though in very different ways, it is taught by the great religions that the 'grubby little human ego' is a fallen and sin-bound creature, alienated from its true ground and destiny; or that it is a self-positing illusion within *maya* or within the pain-ridden process of *samsara*. And in each case it is taught that the present grasping ego must learn to renounce itself, and to give up its claim on existence, in order to enter into the life that is eternal.

There are of course many important differences among the conceptions of the eschaton developed by the different religions. In Hinduism there is both the advaitist conception of total reabsorption of spirits, now divided by innumerable false ego-boundaries, back into the one spirit or atman, which is identical with the ultimate reality of Brahman; and there is also the visiṣṭādvaitist conception of some kind of continuous strands of creaturely identity within the infinite divine life. Buddhism likewise embraces a range of understandings of *nirvāṇa* from sheer non-existence to participation in the eternal but indescribable Void or Absolute. In Christianity there is both the picture of the perfected saints dwelling as separate individuals in the Heavenly City or Kingdom, and the more mystical anticipation of absorption in the beatific vision of God. Such a range of pictures is in no way surprising, since conceptions of humanity's ultimate state can only be pointers to something totally beyond our present experience. However, these different conceptions can I think be seen to be convergent; and one way of indicating the convergence is offered by the modern understanding of personality as essentially self-transcending and interpersonal. From this point of view the fulfilment of human personality cannot consist in the perfection of isolated units, but on the contrary in their transcending of their ego-boundaries in a perfect community of mutual love. Christian thought possesses in the Trinitarian concept of God as three-in-one and one-in-three an illuminating model for such personal multiplicity in unity. Perhaps in the eschaton human existence will be many-in-one and one-in-many in the life of corporate humanity. But whether or not this model is appropriate there is, surely, general agreement that it is not our present little ego, held together by greedy self-concern, that is to be part of the eternal outcome of the temporal process, but rather that which we can eventually become; and that which we can eventually become lies far beyond individual egoity.

And then a third theme in the teachings of the great world religions is that, whilst the ultimate goal is a state in which individual ego-boundaries have been transcended, yet to attain to this the present conscious ego must voluntarily relinquish its own self-centred existence; and the function of religion is to carry men and women through this momentous choice. It is in the sinful 'fallen' creature, or the false ego, which now exists that the conscious exercise of freedom is taking place; and it is therefore to this present imperfect self that the claims and promises of the gospel are addressed. For, whilst the greater life that is available to us is always apprehended as a prevenient reality or as a gift of divine grace, it nevertheless has to be received by men and women as they actually are or as they will actually become in the course of their further living. The greater life, if it is to come about, has to be accepted by the 'grubby little egos' of human beings immersed in the multifarious pressures of history. The great choice is normally made through innumerable small choices. And the unique set of human interactions in time, which we call history, is the sphere within which these vital choices are made. Accordingly, the kind of belief in a life after death which I shall now argue is required by a religious understanding of life is one which postulates a further history, a post-mortem history, in which the work of attaining to self-transcendence is continued to its completion.

In developing this argument let us move from the very general statements that have to be made when we are speaking of the religions of the world collectively, to the more specific statements that we can make in the context of a particular religion, namely Christianity. And indeed since Christianity is itself so diverse I shall be using as my theological framework one particular strand. This is the tradition of reflection which goes back through much contemporary and recent thinking to the great figure of Schleiermacher in the nineteenth century, and ultimately back to the Hellenistic Fathers, particularly Irenaeus, in the second century. According to this type of theology, human existence as we know it is a phase in the cosmic process which is God's gradual creation of 'children of God' – that is, finite personal life lived consciously and joyfully within the infinite divine life. Irenaeus, and others of the Hellenistic Fathers, thought in terms of a two-stage creation of the human being. The first stage – putting it in modern terms – was the production through the evolution of the universe and the evolution of life on this earth (and perhaps on many other planets of many other stars as well) of finite moral and spiritual consciousness. But the human creature thus made as intelligent ethical animal, with a potentiality for relationship with God, is only the raw material for the second phase of the creative process, which is the bringing of men and women, through their own free personal responses, to perfect humanity in relation to God. In Irenaeus's terminology, drawn from Genesis 1:26, humanity has been made in the image of God and is now being drawn into the finite likeness of God. The terminology itself is artificial; but Irenaeus's basic theological hypothesis remains extremely fruitful – namely, an immense creative process, in the first phase of which the human being is not the ideal pre-fallen paradisal Adam and Eve of the Augustinian theology, but is to be thought of as an immature, child-like creature who is only at the beginning of a long further process of development.

Now if our present life is being lived within this second phase, in which intelligent animals are gradually being transformed into children of God, we can very properly ask whether the process is confined to our earthly life or continues beyond it.

It is, I think, obvious and non-controversial that such a transformation, if it is indeed taking place, is not normally completed in the present life. Most human beings are still extremely imperfect as moral and spiritual persons by the time they die. Even when they die at the end of a long and humanly successful life they are still far short of the complete realisation of the human potential; and of course the majority of all those who have been born throughout human history until now have in fact died in infancy or before reaching maturity, or have not lived 'humanly successful' lives. The question then is whether our ultimate perfection, which is so obviously not attained in this life, is to be accomplished in a flash at each individual's death or whether it requires further living beyond death.

The very serious drawback of any notion of instantaneous perfecting at the moment of death is that it would render pointless the slow and difficult process of personal growth through our own free reactions within the contingencies of human history. For if that large part of our perfecting which does not occur in this life is able to be accomplished instantaneously by divine fiat, without our needing freely to go through the intermediate stages, it seems to follow that God could have created humanity initially as the perfect beings whom God wished to have. The traditional way of escape from this conclusion provided by the Augustinian theology is of course the doctrine that God did create perfect creatures – the angels – in an ideal state, but that some of them willfully rebelled. But it has long been evident that this speculation is incoherent; for perfect creatures in a perfect environment, although free to fall, would never in fact do so. Either, then, the experience of living and learning within a challenging environment is necessary to the creation of free personal beings who are to be 'children of God' – in which case it would seem that the creative process must continue beyond death until it is completed; or else that kind of experience and exercise of free will is not necessary because God can equally well create perfect children 'ready made' – in which case there is no point or justification to the long story of human existence, with all the deep pain and suffering that it involves.

Surely this second alternative rules itself out by the way in which it would render our present struggling human existence pointless. We must then proceed on the basis that life as we know it is part of a long person-making process which is not completed in this present life and which we can only presume to continue beyond it. This presumption is confirmed by the insight of the Eastern religions that spiritual 'liberation' requires far more than one life for its achievement. They accordingly teach the reincarnation of the soul in life after life until ego-hood is finally transcended. In the West most of us have not accepted this doctrine of earthly reincarnation or rebirth; and, whilst the subject is much too large to be discussed properly here, I think that we have respectable reasons (which I have tried to discuss elsewhere[7]) for our cautious and on the whole negative response. But nevertheless the perception that one life is not enough is surely sound. I would therefore suggest that if we accept (1) the witness of the great world religions that human existence as we now know it is 'fallen', wrapped in illusion, full of suffering; and (2) that nevertheless a far, far better state is possible, a state of perfection, fulfilment, as child of God; and (3) that this state cannot be simply imposed upon us but has to be freely entered into through innumerable choices of self-transcendence; and (4) that this process is not normally completed in the present life – then we should also accept the unanimous witness of the great religious traditions to a further life or lives beyond death.

Accordingly, in addition to eschatology, concerned with the ultimate and eternal state to which the religions point, there is also what we may call pareschatology, concerned with what takes place between this present life and that final state. The pareschaton is the time in which the individual changes from a still self-centred state at the end of this life, to one of the transcendence of egoity within the unity of perfected humanity living in an ideal relationship to God. The main form of pareschatology in Christian thought is of course the Catholic doctrine of purgatory. Unfortunately this has traditionally been combined with the dogma that the soul's relationship to God is settled in the moment of death, so that there can thereafter be no further vital free choices or personal growth and development. Thus purgatory as traditionally conceived is not a continued life of moral responses to other people within a common environment through which the self can continue to grow towards its perfection. It has been conceived, rather, as the process through which the soul, already definitively 'saved' in the moment of death, endures the remaining painful consequences of its earthly sins and is thus made fit to enter the Heavenly Kingdom. But this is essentially a juridical conception, concerned with the judgment of the person at a particular moment, regardless of his or her individual circumstances and development. I suggest that such a scheme of divine judgement is not a morally coherent possibility. It would be manifestly unfair to judge men and women and allot them eternal happiness or loss of happiness on the basis of their performance in this life and/or their state at the moment of death. For people are born, through no virtue or fault of their own, in circumstances of very different moral and spiritual advantage. There are immense variations of genetic make-up, and at least as great variations in the moral character of the environments into which people are born. Consider the contrast between, on the one hand, a child born to good, loving and moderately affluent parents and brought up in an atmosphere of religious faith within a settled and stable society, and, on the other hand, an orphan deprived of all parental affection and guidance, living in the teeming slums of an overcrowded and vice-ridden city in which he or she is subjected to a variety of vicious influences, is part of a sub-culture in which crime is a way of life and dies a violent death at the age of seventeen. To judge them both on the moral quality of their lives would be patently unjust. Again, the state in which someone is at the moment of death would provide only a very haphazard criterion since death may come unexpectedly at any time. It is thus surely very difficult to conceive of the divine Being distributing human beings to eternal happiness or unhappiness (or, on a milder view of divine rejection, simply ceasing to hold them in existence) on the basis of their performance in this brief and chancy life. Rather than such a harsh juridical approach, does it not seem more appropriate to think in terms of the actual nature and quality of human existence as it changes through time, and to postulate a divine purpose of drawing men and women towards the realisation of their God-given potentialities? Since any such purpose is obviously not fulfilled in the present life it would seem that it must continue beyond this life. But in that case the pareschaton will not be the spiritually static purgatory of Catholic tradition, but is more likely to be a further temporal process in which further moral and spiritual growth is possible.

If I am challenged to say more about what this might mean, I can only offer one or two very tentative first steps of speculation, guided partly by the evidence of religious and other experience and partly by what seem to me to be rational likelihoods.

I am assuming then that when the physical organism dies the conscious personality continues to exist. And I speculate that in the first phase of its post-mortem existence it is not embodied, and accordingly receives no new sensory input, but experiences a kind of dream environment built out of the materials of memory by the moulding power of conscious and repressed desires developed in the course of its earthly life. This will be a period of self-revelation and self-judgement, a kind of psychoanalytic experience in which we become aware of our own character so largely hidden from us in this life, and perhaps as a result form new and different hopes and aspirations. This conception of the first phase of existence after death is based on the Tantric Mahāyanā document the *Bardo Thödol* or *Tibetan Book of the Dead*. For what it is worth – and it is I think very hard to decide what, if anything, it is worth – the reports, received through Western mediums, purporting to reflect the experiences of persons who have recently died, agree generally with the *Bardo Thödol*. For it is explicit in this ancient document that the *bardo* experience is a projection of the individual's own imagination, so that its form depends upon that person's operative beliefs and expectations. The *Bardo Thödol* describes the post-mortem experiences which would be undergone by a devout Tibetan Buddhist. But a member of our post-Christian Western secular society might well, in default of any strong religious imagery, create his or her *bardo* world out of memories of earth, so that such a next world would be very like the present world; and this is in fact generally what is indicated by the minds which express themselves in the mediumistic trance.

Then I speculate that after this *bardo* phase, which lasts for a longer or shorter time according to the needs of the individual, there is another period of embodiment, which Christians antici-pate as the resurrection. This is a bodily existence lived in interaction with other people in a common environment. The resurrection environment, including the bodies which are part of it, is physical though probably not part of the physical universe of which our present bodies are part. Thus we may well have to postulate a plurality of universes or spatial systems. There are of course formidable philosophical problems about personal iden-tity from embodiment in one space to re-embodiment in another space. I have tried to confront these problems elsewhere,[8] but the questions involved are too intricate to be tackled adequately in the closing stages of this lecture. I would only suggest to anyone who takes the idea of resurrection or re-embodiment seriously enough to consider how it might be spelled out that no realistic alternative has yet been offered to the idea of a further psycho-physical existence which is probably located in another space.

If we are allowed to speculate this far we have a hypothetical basis on which to speculate yet a little further. The reason for postulating a life after death, within the theological framework adopted here, is that it is entailed by the possibility of human beings exercising their freedom in response to the challenges and opportunities of history so as to be able to attain eventually to the point of self-transcending life in a universal perfected humanity. Accordingly, the form of post-mortem existence that we postulate must be one in which further moral and spiritual choices are possible. This means, I think, that it must be a real life in a real world with its own concrete character and history, and with its own exigencies and crises and perils within which decisions and risks, successes and failures, achievements and disasters can occur. All this points to the hypothesis that the individual's next life will, like the present life, be a bounded span with its own beginning and end. In other words I am suggesting that it will be another mortal existence. For it is our mortality that gives to our present life its shape and meaning. It is because of the boundaries of birth and death that time is precious, that right and wrong actions have their momentous character within the irreversible flow of events, and that life can have the kind of meaning that presupposes aims and purposes. It is indeed very hard to see how a finite and imperfect human person could undergo further development except within a temporal horizon such as death provides.

The next question that arises is whether we should postulate only one such further bounded life or more than one. We have to consider this in relation to the creation of an eschatological situation in which the innumerable human individuals have reached a self-transcending relationship to one another, constituting a new humanity which is many-in-one and one-in-many. It is evident that this is very far from being achieved in the present life; and it therefore seems more realistic to think of its coming about at the end of a number of lives than to see this happening at the end of only one more. We are thus led – very tentatively – to postulate a series of lives, presumably in a corresponding series of worlds, through which finite persons can gradually progress towards the completion of the divine purpose for them.

To those whose religious thinking is conducted entirely within the borders of the Christian tradition, such speculations will almost inevitably seem wild and baseless. For if one's experience is confined to one's own familiar conceptual village the life of other villages will seem merely alien and bizarre. But those who are aware of the wider religious life of humankind will recognise that the present speculation is a variation on the very ancient and widespread conception of a multiplicity of lives – except that, where Buddhism and Hinduism, as the principal channels of this tradition, teach a horizontal process of reincarnation along the plane of earthly history, I have been outlining what might be called a vertical, or perhaps better a diagonal, series of many lives in many worlds, moving nearer to the divine heart of reality. And I speculate that, as human beings reach their final self-transcending perfection, the life in which this occurs becomes their last embodiment and they pass from it into *nirvāṇa* or heaven or eternal life, beyond separate egoity in space and time.

You have perhaps noticed that I have spoken much of the soul's progress but very little of its regress. I nevertheless assume that at every stage regress is possible as well as progress and that the total journey of the self from human animal to child of God is no smooth and automatic ascent but a hard and adventurous journey with many ups and downs and stops and starts. I do however also assume eventual 'universal salvation'. This assumption provokes large problems, particularly concerning the relation between an ultimate predestination to salvation and the genuine human freedom which I have also stressed. But this is another large topic which I have discussed at length elsewhere.[9]

Finally, a very brief word about method. It will be evident that the speculations which I have outlined unite some of the basic features of the eschatologies and pareschatologies of both West and East. And it does seem to me to be an appropriate and fruitful method today to assume that the teachings of the world religions express different human perceptions of and responses to the same divine Reality, so that a fuller conception of that reality, and likewise of human destiny in relation to it, is to be expected from religious study on a global scale than from study restricted to a single tradition.

NOTES

1. Jürgen Moltmann, *Theology of Hope* (London: SCM, 1967) p. 16.
2. Wolfhart Pannenberg, 'Can Christianity Do Without an Eschatology?', in *The Christian Hope*, ed. G. B. Caird *et al.* (London: SPCK, 1970) p. 31.
3. John Hick, *Death and Eternal Life* (London: Collins; New York: Harper and Row, 1976. New edition, London: Macmillan, 1985) ch. 11.

4. Wolfhart Pannenberg, *What is Man?* (Philadelphia: Fortress Press, 1970) p. 48.

5. Wolfhart Pannenberg, *Jesus – God and Man* (London: SCM, 1968) p. 87.

6. Gordon D. Kaufman, *Systematic Theology* (New York: Charles Scribner's Sons, 1968) p. 464.

7. Hick, *Death and Eternal Life*, ch. 19.

8. Ibid., ch. 15.

9. Ibid., ch. 13.

Index